Rule Book of Games
Badminton

Leonida Weatherford

Alpha Editions

ISBN : 9789352976928

Design and Setting By

Alpha Editions

email - alphaedis@gmail.com

Contents

Preface

Badminton is a racquet sport played using racquets to hit a shuttlecock across a net. Although it may be played with larger teams, the most common forms of the game are "singles" (with one player per side) and "doubles" (with two players per side). Badminton is often played as a casual outdoor activity in a yard or on a beach; formal games are played on a rectangular indoor court. Points are scored by striking the shuttlecock with the racquet and landing it within the opposing side's half of the court.

Each side may only strike the shuttlecock once before it passes over the net. Play ends once the shuttlecock has struck the floor or if a fault has been called by the umpire, service judge, or (in their absence) the opposing side.

The shuttlecock is a feathered or (in informal matches) plastic projectile which flies differently from the balls used in many other sports. In particular, the feathers create much higher drag, causing the shuttlecock to decelerate more rapidly. Shuttlecocks also have a high top speed compared to the balls in other racquet sports. The flight of the shuttlecock gives the sport its distinctive nature.

Badminton racquets are lightweight, with top quality racquets weighing between 70 and 95 grams (2.5 and 3.4 ounces) not including grip or strings. They are composed of many different materials ranging from carbon fibre composite (graphite reinforced plastic) to solid steel, which may be augmented by a variety of materials. Carbon fibre has an excellent strength to weight ratio, is stiff, and gives excellent kinetic energy transfer. Before the adoption of carbon fibre composite, racquets were made of light metals such as aluminium. Earlier still, racquets were made of wood. Cheap racquets are still often made of metals such as steel, but wooden racquets are no longer manufactured for the ordinary market, because of their excessive mass and cost. Nowadays, nanomaterials such as carbon nanotubes and fullerene are added to racquets giving them greater durability.

The most fundamental aspect of badminton technique is the grip. The grip is how a badminton holds the badminton racket. A correct grip is a pathway for a badminton player to improve upon their skills. on the contrary, using an incorrect grip is often a brickwall that leads to poor form and poorly executed techniques. It takes much more time to unlearn a bad technique than to learn one. Many of us have experienced it before the painful way. The proper badminton grips may feel uncomfortable and unnatural in the beginning, but if you are able to get over that fact, later on you will appreciate what you have learned.

Serving is arguably the most important aspect of the game, as it is the one shot which has to be in every single rally. You have as much time as you need to get ready for it, so there is no excuse for not getting it right. Here we demonstrate and explain three basic types of serve - high server, low serve and flick serve. Good serves put opponents under pressure, and give servers a better opportunity for success. There are 3 basic serves; High Serve (used in singles only, Low Serve (used in both singles and doubles) and Flick serve (used in doubles).

This is a reference book. All the matter is just compiled and edited in nature, taken from the various sources which are in public domain.

This book features an enormous amount of information about Badminton throughout the world. This is a comprehensive text, offering both beginners and advanced Badminton players the knowledge necessary to play this sport.

—*Editor*

1

Badminton

Badminton is a racquet sport played using racquets to hit a shuttlecock across a net. Although it may be played with larger teams, the most common forms of the game are "singles" (with one player per side) and "doubles" (with two players per side). Badminton is often played as a casual outdoor activity in a yard or on a beach; formal games are played on a rectangular indoor court. Points are scored by striking the shuttlecock with the racquet and landing it within the opposing side's half of the court.

Each side may only strike the shuttlecock once before it passes over the net. Play ends once the shuttlecock has struck the floor or if a fault has been called by the umpire, service judge, or (in their absence) the opposing side.

The shuttlecock is a feathered or (in informal matches) plastic projectile which flies differently from the balls used in many other sports. In particular, the feathers create much higher drag, causing the shuttlecock to decelerate more rapidly. Shuttlecocks also have a high top speed compared to the balls in other racquet sports. The flight of the shuttlecock gives the sport its distinctive nature.

The game developed in British India from the earlier game of battledore and shuttlecock. European play came to be dominated by Denmark but the game has become very popular in Asia, with recent competitions dominated by China. Since 1992, badminton has been a Summer Olympic sport with four events: men's singles, women's singles, men's doubles, and women's doubles, with mixed doubles added four years later. At high levels of play, the sport demands excellent fitness: players require aerobic stamina, agility, strength, speed, and precision. It is also a technical sport, requiring good motor coordination and the development of sophisticated racquet movements.

HISTORY

Games employing shuttlecocks have been played for centuries across Eurasia, but the modern game of badminton developed in the mid-19th century among the British as a variant of the earlier game of battledore and shuttlecock. ("Battledore" was an older term for "racquet".)

Its exact origin remains obscure. The name derives from the Duke of Beaufort's Badminton House in Gloucestershire, but why or when remains unclear. As early as 1860, a London toy dealer named Isaac Spratt published a booklet entitled *Badminton Battledore – A New Game*, but no copy is known to have survived. An 1863 article in *The Cornhill Magazine* describes badminton as "battledore and shuttlecock played with sides, across a string suspended some five feet from the ground".

The game may have originally developed among expatriate officers in British India, where it was very popular by the 1870s. Ball badminton, a form of the game played with a wool ball instead of a shuttlecock, was being played in Thanjavur as early as the 1850s and was at first played interchangeably with badminton by the British, the woollen ball being preferred in windy or wet weather.

Early on, the game was also known as Poona or Poonah after the garrison town of Pune, where it was particularly popular and where the first rules for the game were drawn up in 1873. By 1875, officers returning home had started a badminton club in Folkestone. Initially, the sport was played with sides ranging from 1 to 4 players, but it was quickly established that games between two or four competitors worked the best. The shuttlecocks were coated with India rubber and, in outdoor play, sometimes weighted with lead. Although the depth of the net was of no consequence, it was preferred that it should reach the ground.

The sport was played under the Pune rules until 1887, when J. H. E. Hart of the Bath Badminton Club drew up revised regulations. In 1890, Hart and Bagnel Wild again revised the rules.

The Badminton Association of England (BAE) published these rules in 1893 and officially launched the sport at a house called "Dunbar" in Portsmouth on 13 September. The BAE started the first badminton competition, the All England Open Badminton Championships for gentlemen's doubles, ladies' doubles, and mixed doubles, in 1899. Singles competitions were added in 1900 and an England–Ireland championship match appeared in 1904.

England, Scotland, Wales, Canada, Denmark, France, Ireland, the Netherlands, and New Zealand were the founding members of the International Badminton Federation in 1934, now known as the Badminton World Federation. India joined as an affiliate in 1936. The BWF now governs international badminton. Although initiated in England, competitive men's badminton has traditionally been dominated in Europe by Denmark. Worldwide, Asian nations have become dominant in international competition. China, Denmark, India, Indonesia, Malaysia, and South Korea are the nations which have consistently produced world-class players in the past few decades, with China being the greatest force in men's and women's competition recently.

The game has also become a popular backyard sport in the United States.

RULES

The following information is a simplified summary of badminton rules based on the BWF Statutes publication, *Laws of Badminton*.

Court

The court is rectangular and divided into halves by a net. Courts are usually marked for both singles and doubles play, although badminton rules permit a court to be marked for singles only. The doubles court is wider than the singles court, but both are of the same length. The exception, which often causes confusion to newer players, is that the doubles court has a shorter serve-length dimension.

The full width of the court is 6.1 metres (20 ft), and in singles this width is reduced to 5.18 metres (17 ft). The full length of the court is 13.4 metres (44 ft). The service courts are marked by a centre line dividing the width of the court, by a short service line at a distance of 1.98 metres (6 ft 6 inch) from the net, and by the outer side and back boundaries. In doubles, the service court is also marked by a long service line, which is 0.76 metres (2 ft 6 inch) from the back boundary.

The net is 1.55 metres (5 ft 1 inch) high at the edges and 1.524 metres (5 ft) high in the centre. The net posts are placed over the doubles sidelines, even when singles is played.

The minimum height for the ceiling above the court is not mentioned in the Laws of Badminton. Nonetheless, a badminton court will not be suitable if the ceiling is likely to be hit on a high serve.

Serving

When the server serves, the shuttlecock must pass over the short service line on the opponents' court or it will count as a fault.

At the start of the rally, the server and receiver stand in diagonally opposite *service courts*. The server hits the shuttlecock so that it would land in the receiver's service court. This is similar to tennis, except that a badminton serve must be hit below waist height and with the racquet shaft pointing downwards, the shuttlecock is not allowed to bounce and in badminton, the players stand inside their service courts, unlike tennis.

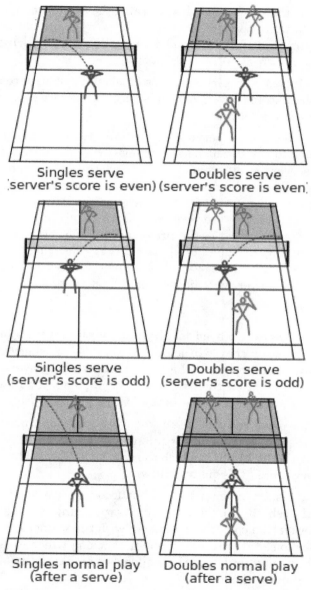

Singles serve
(server's score is even)

Doubles serve
(server's score is even)

Singles serve
(server's score is odd)

Doubles serve
(server's score is odd)

Singles normal play
(after a serve)

Doubles normal play
(after a serve)

The legal bounds of a badminton court during various stages of a rally for singles and doubles games

When the serving side loses a rally, the server immediately passes to their opponent(s) (this differs from the old system where sometimes the serve passes to the doubles partner for what is known as a "second serve").

In singles, the server stands in their right service court when their score is even, and in her/his left service court when her/his score is odd.

In doubles, if the serving side wins a rally, the same player continues to serve, but he/she changes service courts so that she/he serves to a different opponent each time. If the opponents win the rally and their new score is even, the player in the right service court serves; if odd, the player in the left service court serves. The players' service courts are determined by their positions at the start of the previous rally, not by where they were standing at the end of the rally. A consequence of this system is that each time a side regains the service, the server will be the player who did *not* serve last time.

Scoring

Each game is played to 21 points, with players scoring a point whenever they win a rally regardless of whether they served (this differs from the old system where players could only win a point on their serve and each game was played to 15 points). A match is the best of three games.

If the score reaches 20-all, then the game continues until one side gains a two-point lead (such as 24–22), except when there is a tie at 29-all, in which the game goes to a golden point. Whoever scores this point will win.

At the start of a match, the shuttlecock is cast and the side towards which the shuttlecock is pointing serves first. Alternatively, a coin may be tossed, with the winners choosing whether to serve or receive first, or choosing which end of the court to occupy first, and their opponents making the leftover the remaining choice.

In subsequent games, the winners of the previous game serve first. Matches are best out of three: a player or pair must win two games (of 21 points each) to win the match. For the first rally of any doubles game, the serving pair may decide who serves and the receiving pair may decide who receives. The players change ends at the start of the second game; if the match reaches a third game, they change ends both at the start of the game and when the leading player's or pair's score reaches 11 points.

The server and receiver must remain within their service courts, without touching the boundary lines, until the server strikes the shuttlecock. The other two players may stand wherever they wish, so long as they do not block the vision of the server or receiver.

Lets

If a let is called, the rally is stopped and replayed with no change to the score. Lets may occur because of some unexpected disturbance such as a shuttlecock landing on a court (having been hit there by players playing in adjacent court) or in small halls the shuttle may touch an overhead rail which can be classed as a let.

If the receiver is not ready when the service is delivered, a let shall be called; yet, if the receiver attempts to return the shuttlecock, the receiver shall be judged to have been ready.

EQUIPMENT

Badminton rules restrict the design and size of racquets and shuttlecocks.

Racquets

Badminton racquets are lightweight, with top quality racquets weighing between 70 and 95 grams (2.5 and 3.4 ounces) not including grip or strings. They are composed of many different materials ranging from carbon fibre composite (graphite reinforced plastic) to solid steel, which may be augmented by a variety of materials. Carbon fibre has an excellent strength to weight ratio, is stiff, and gives excellent kinetic energy transfer. Before the adoption of carbon fibre composite, racquets were made of light metals such as aluminium. Earlier still, racquets were made of wood. Cheap racquets are still often made of metals such as steel, but wooden racquets are no longer manufactured for the ordinary market, because of their excessive mass and cost. Nowadays, nanomaterials such as carbon nanotubes and fullerene are added to racquets giving them greater durability.

There is a wide variety of racquet designs, although the laws limit the racquet size and shape. Different racquets have playing characteristics that appeal to different players. The traditional oval head shape is still available, but an isometric head shape is increasingly common in new racquets.

Strings

Badminton strings are thin, high performing strings with thicknesses ranging from about 0.62 to 0.73 mm. Thicker strings are more durable, but many players prefer the feel of thinner strings. String tension is normally in the range of 80 to 160 N (18 to 36 lbf). Recreational players generally string at lower tensions than professionals, typically between 80 and 110 N (18 and 25 lbf). Professionals string between about 110 and 160 N (25 and 36 lbf). Some string manufacturers measure the thickness of their strings under tension so they are actually thicker than specified when slack. Ashaway Micropower is actually 0.7mm but Yonex BG-66 is about 0.72mm.

It is often argued that high string tensions improve control, whereas low string tensions increase power. The arguments for this generally rely on crude mechanical reasoning, such as claiming that a lower tension string bed is more bouncy and therefore provides more power. This is, in fact, incorrect, for a higher string tension can cause the shuttle to slide off the racquet and hence make it harder to hit a shot accurately. An alternative view suggests that the optimum tension for power depends on the player: the faster and more accurately a player can swing their racquet, the higher the tension for maximum power. Neither view has been subjected to a rigorous mechanical analysis, nor is there clear evidence in favour of one or the other. The most effective way for a player to find a good string tension is to experiment.

Grip

The choice of grip allows a player to increase the thickness of their racquet handle and choose a comfortable surface to hold. A player may build up the handle with one or several grips before applying the final layer.

Players may choose between a variety of grip materials. The most common choices are PU synthetic grips or towelling grips. Grip choice is a matter of personal preference. Players often find that sweat becomes a problem; in this case, a drying agent may be applied to the grip or hands, sweatbands may be used, the player may choose another grip material or change his/her grip more frequently.

There are two main types of grip: *replacement* grips and *overgrips*. Replacement grips are thicker and are often used to increase the size of the handle. Overgrips are thinner (less than 1 mm), and are often used as the final layer. Many players, however, prefer to use replacement grips as the final layer. Towelling grips are always replacement grips. Replacement grips have an adhesive backing, whereas overgrips have only a small patch of adhesive at the start of the tape and must be applied under tension; overgrips are more convenient for players who change grips frequently, because they may be removed more rapidly without damaging the underlying material.

Shuttlecock

A shuttlecock (often abbreviated to *shuttle*; also called a *birdie*) is a high-drag projectile, with an open conical shape: the cone is formed from sixteen overlapping feathers embedded into a rounded cork base. The cork is covered with thin leather or synthetic material. Synthetic shuttles are often used by recreational players to reduce their costs as feathered shuttles break easily. These nylon shuttles may be constructed with either natural cork or synthetic foam base and a plastic skirt.

A shuttlecock with a plastic skirt

Badminton rules also provide for testing a shuttlecock for the correct speed:

1. To test a shuttlecock, hit a full underhand stroke which makes contact with the shuttlecock over the back boundary line. The shuttlecock shall be hit at an upward angle and in a direction parallel to the sidelines.

2. A shuttlecock of the correct speed will land not less than 530 mm and not more than 990 mm short of the other back boundary line.

Shoes

Badminton shoes are lightweight with soles of rubber or similar high-grip, non-marking materials.

Compared to running shoes, badminton shoes have little lateral support. High levels of lateral support are useful for activities where lateral motion is undesirable and unexpected. Badminton, however, requires powerful lateral movements. A highly built-up lateral support will not be able to protect the foot in badminton; instead, it will encourage catastrophic collapse at the point where the shoe's support fails, and the player's ankles are not ready for the sudden loading, which can cause sprains. For this reason, players should choose badminton shoes rather than general trainers or running shoes, because proper badminton shoes will have a very thin sole, lower a person's centre of gravity, and therefore result in fewer injuries. Players should also ensure that they learn safe and proper footwork, with the knee and foot in alignment on all lunges. This is more than just a safety concern: proper footwork is also critical in order to move effectively around the court.

TECHNIQUE

A female player flies high in USA, 2006

Strokes

Badminton offers a wide variety of basic strokes, and players require a high level of skill to perform all of them effectively.

All strokes can be played either *forehand* or *backhand*. A player's forehand side is the same side as their playing hand: for a right-handed player, the forehand side is their right side and the backhand side is their left side. Forehand strokes are hit with the front of the hand leading (like hitting with the palm), whereas backhand strokes are hit with the back of the hand leading (like hitting with the knuckles). Players frequently play certain strokes on the forehand side with a backhand hitting action, and vice versa.

In the forecourt and midcourt, most strokes can be played equally effectively on either the forehand or backhand side; but in the rear court, players will attempt to play as many strokes as possible on their forehands, often preferring to play a *round-the-head* forehand overhead (a forehand "on the backhand side") rather than attempt a backhand overhead. Playing a backhand overhead has two main disadvantages. First, the player must turn their back to their opponents, restricting their view of them and the court. Second, backhand overheads cannot be hit with as much power as forehands: the hitting action is limited by the shoulder joint, which permits a much greater range of movement for a forehand overhead than for a backhand. The *backhand clear* is considered by most players and coaches to be the most difficult basic stroke in the game, since the precise technique is needed in order to muster enough power for the shuttlecock to travel the full length of the court. For the same reason, *backhand smashes* tend to be weak.

Position of the shuttlecock and receiving player

The choice of stroke depends on how near the shuttlecock is to the net, whether it is above net height, and where an opponent is currently positioned: players have much better attacking options if they can reach the shuttlecock well above net height, especially if it is also close to the net. In the forecourt, a high shuttlecock will be met with a *net kill*, hitting it steeply downwards and attempting to win the rally immediately. This is why it is best to drop the shuttlecock just over the net in this situation.

A player does a forehand service, 2009, Philadelphia

In the midcourt, a high shuttlecock will usually be met with a powerful *smash*, also hitting downwards and hoping for an outright winner or a weak reply. Athletic *jump smashes*, where players jump upwards for a steeper smash angle, are a common and spectacular element of elite men's doubles play.

In the rearcourt, players strive to hit the shuttlecock while it is still above them, rather than allowing it to drop lower. This *overhead* hitting allows them to play smashes, *clears* (hitting the shuttlecock high and to the back of the opponents' court), and *drop shots* (hitting the shuttlecock softly so that it falls sharply downwards into the opponents' forecourt).

If the shuttlecock has dropped lower, then a smash is impossible and a full-length, high clear is difficult.

Vertical position of the shuttlecock

A player prepares for a vertical jump smash

When the shuttlecock is well below net height, players have no choice but to hit upwards. *Lifts*, where the shuttlecock is hit upwards to the back of the opponents' court, can be played from all parts of the court.

If a player does not lift, his only remaining option is to push the shuttlecock softly back to the net: in the forecourt, this is called a *net shot*; in the midcourt or rear court, it is often called a *push* or *block*.

When the shuttlecock is near to net height, players can hit *drives*, which travel flat and rapidly over the net into the opponents' rear midcourt and rear court. Pushes may also be hit flatter, placing the shuttlecock into the front midcourt. Drives and pushes may be played from the midcourt or forecourt, and are most often used in doubles: they are an attempt to regain the attack, rather than choosing to lift the shuttlecock and defend against smashes. After a successful drive or push, the opponents will often be forced to lift the shuttlecock.

Spin

Balls may be spun to alter their bounce (for example, topspin and backspin in tennis) or trajectory, and players may slice the ball (strike it with an angled racquet face) to produce such spin. The shuttlecock is not allowed to bounce, but slicing the shuttlecock does have applications in badminton.

- Slicing the shuttlecock from the side may cause it to travel in a different direction from the direction suggested by the player's racquet or body movement. This is used to deceive opponents.

- Slicing the shuttlecock from the side may cause it to follow a slightly curved path (as seen from above), and the deceleration imparted by the spin causes sliced strokes to slow down more suddenly towards the end of their flight path. This can be used to create drop shots and smashes that dip more steeply after they pass the net.

- When playing a net shot, slicing underneath the shuttlecock may cause it to turn over itself (tumble) several times as it passes the net. This is called a *spinning net shot* or *tumbling net shot*. The opponent will be unwilling to address the shuttlecock until it has corrected its orientation.

Due to the way that its feathers overlap, a shuttlecock also has a slight natural spin about its axis of rotational symmetry. The spin is in a counter-clockwise direction as seen from above when dropping a shuttlecock. This natural spin affects certain strokes: a tumbling net shot is more effective if the slicing action is from right to left, rather than from left to right.

Biomechanics

Badminton biomechanics have not been the subject of extensive scientific study, but some studies confirm the minor role of the wrist in power generation and indicate that the major contributions to power come from internal and external rotations of the upper and lower arm. Recent guides to the sport thus emphasize forearm rotation rather than wrist movements.

The feathers impart substantial drag, causing the shuttlecock to decelerate greatly over distance. The shuttlecock is also extremely aerodynamically stable: regardless of initial orientation, it will turn to fly cork-first and remain in the cork-first orientation. One consequence of the shuttlecock's drag is that it requires considerable power to hit it the full length of the court, which is not the case for most racquet sports. The drag also influences the flight path of a lifted (*lobbed*) shuttlecock: the parabola of its flight is heavily skewed so that it falls at a steeper angle than it rises. With very high serves, the shuttlecock may even fall vertically.

Other factors

When defending against a smash, players have three basic options: lift, block, or drive. In singles, a block to the net is the most common reply. In doubles, a lift is the safest option but it usually allows the opponents to continue smashing; blocks and drives are counter-attacking strokes but may be intercepted by the smasher's partner. Many players use a backhand hitting action for returning smashes on both the forehand and backhand sides because backhands are more effective than forehands at covering smashes directed to the body. Hard shots directed towards the body are difficult to defend.

The service is restricted by the Laws and presents its own array of stroke choices. Unlike in tennis, the server's racquet must be pointing in a downward direction to deliver the serve so normally the shuttle must be hit upwards to pass over the net. The server can choose a *low serve* into the forecourt (like a push), or a lift to the back of the service court, or a flat *drive serve*. Lifted serves may be either *high serves*, where the shuttlecock is lifted so high that it falls almost vertically at the back of the court, or *flick serves*, where the shuttlecock is lifted to a lesser height but falls sooner.

Deception

Once players have mastered these basic strokes, they can hit the shuttlecock from and to any part of the court, powerfully and softly as required. Beyond the basics, however, badminton offers rich potential for advanced stroke skills that provide a competitive advantage. Because badminton players have to cover a short distance as quickly as possible, the purpose of many advanced strokes is to deceive the opponent, so that either he is tricked into believing that a different stroke is being played, or he is forced to delay his movement until he actually sees the shuttle's direction. "Deception" in badminton is often used in both of these senses. When a player is genuinely deceived, he will often lose the point immediately because he cannot change his direction quickly enough to reach the shuttlecock. Experienced players will be aware of the trick and cautious not to move too early, but the attempted deception is still useful because it forces the opponent to delay his movement slightly. Against weaker players whose intended strokes are obvious, an experienced player may move before the shuttlecock has been hit, anticipating the stroke to gain an advantage.

Slicing and using a *shortened hitting action* are the two main technical devices that facilitate deception. Slicing involves hitting the shuttlecock with an angled racquet face, causing it to travel in a different direction than suggested by the body or arm movement. Slicing also causes the shuttlecock to travel more slowly than the arm movement suggests. For example, a good crosscourt *sliced drop shot* will use a hitting action that suggests a straight clear or a smash, deceiving the opponent about both the power and direction of the shuttlecock. A more sophisticated slicing action involves brushing the strings around the shuttlecock during the hit, in order to make the shuttlecock spin. This can be used to improve the shuttle's trajectory, by making it dip more rapidly as it passes the net; for example, a sliced low serve can travel slightly faster than a normal low serve, yet land on the same spot. Spinning the shuttlecock is also used to create *spinning net shots* (also called *tumbling net shots*), in which the shuttlecock turns over itself several times (tumbles) before stabilizing; sometimes the shuttlecock remains inverted instead of tumbling. The main advantage of a spinning net shot is that the opponent will be unwilling to address the shuttlecock until it has stopped tumbling, since hitting the feathers will result in an unpredictable stroke. Spinning net shots are especially important for high-level singles players.

The lightness of modern racquets allows players to use a very short hitting action for many strokes, thereby maintaining the option to hit a powerful or a soft stroke until the last possible moment. For example, a singles player may hold his racquet ready for a net shot, but then flick the shuttlecock to the back instead with a shallow lift when she or he notices the opponent has moved before the actual shot was played. A shallow lift takes less time to reach the ground and as mentioned above a rally is over when the shuttlecock touches the ground. This makes the opponent's task of covering the whole court much more difficult than if the lift was hit higher and with a bigger, obvious swing. A short hitting action is not only useful for deception: it also allows the player to hit powerful strokes when he has no time for a big arm swing. A big arm swing is also usually not advised in badminton because bigger swings make it more difficult to recover for the next shot in fast exchanges. The use of grip tightening is crucial to these techniques, and is often described as *finger power*. Elite players develop finger power to the extent that they can hit some power strokes, such as net kills, with less than a 10 centimetres (4 inches) racquet swing.

It is also possible to reverse this style of deception, by suggesting a powerful stroke before slowing down the hitting action to play a soft stroke. In general, this latter style of deception is more common in the rear court (for example, drop shots disguised as smashes), whereas the former style is more common in the forecourt and midcourt (for example, lifts disguised as net shots).

Deception is not limited to slicing and short hitting actions. Players may also use *double motion*, where they make an initial racquet movement in one direction before withdrawing the racquet to hit in another direction. Players will often do this to send opponents in the wrong direction. The racquet movement is typically used to suggest a straight angle but then play the stroke crosscourt, or vice versa. *Triple motion* is also possible, but this is very rare in actual play. An alternative to double motion is to use a *racquet head fake*, where the initial motion is continued but the racquet is turned during the hit. This produces a smaller change in direction but does not require as much time.

STRATEGY

To win in badminton, players need to employ a wide variety of strokes in the right situations. These range from powerful jumping smashes to delicate tumbling net returns. Often rallies finish with a smash, but setting up the smash requires subtler strokes. For example, a net shot can force the opponent to lift the shuttlecock, which gives an opportunity to smash. If the net shot is tight and tumbling, then the opponent's lift will not reach the back of the court, which makes the subsequent smash much harder to return.

Deception is also important. Expert players prepare for many different strokes that look identical and use slicing to deceive their opponents about the speed or direction of the stroke. If an opponent tries to anticipate the stroke, he may move in the wrong direction and may be unable to change his body momentum in time to reach the shuttlecock.

Singles

Since one person needs to cover the entire court, singles tactics are based on forcing the opponent to move as much as possible; this means that singles strokes are normally directed to the corners of the court. Players exploit the length of the court by combining lifts and clears with drop shots and net shots. Smashing tends to be less prominent in singles than in doubles because the smasher has no partner to follow up his effort and is thus vulnerable to a skillfully placed return. Moreover, frequent smashing can be exhausting in singles where the conservation of a player's energy is at a premium. However, players with strong smashes will sometimes use the shot to create openings, and players commonly smash weak returns to try to end rallies.

In singles, players will often start the rally with a forehand high serve or with a flick serve. Low serves are also used frequently, either forehand or backhand. Drive serves are rare.

At high levels of play, singles demand extraordinary fitness. Singles is a game of patient positional manoeuvring, unlike the all-out aggression of doubles.

Doubles

Both pairs will try to gain and maintain the attack, smashing downwards when the opportunity arises. Whenever possible, a pair will adopt an ideal attacking formation with one player hitting down from the rear court, and his partner in the midcourt intercepting all smash returns except the lift. If the rear court attacker plays a drop shot, his partner will move into the forecourt to threaten the net reply. If a pair cannot hit downwards, they will use flat strokes in an attempt to gain the attack. If a pair is forced to lift or clear the shuttlecock, then they must defend: they will adopt a side-by-side position in the rear midcourt, to cover the full width of their court against the opponents' smashes. In doubles, players generally smash to the middle ground between two players in order to take advantage of confusion and clashes.

At high levels of play, the backhand serve has become popular to the extent that forehand serves have become fairly rare at a high level of play. The straight low serve is used most frequently, in an attempt to prevent the opponents gaining the attack immediately. Flick serves are used to prevent the opponent from anticipating the low serve and attacking it decisively.

At high levels of play, doubles rallies are extremely fast. Men's doubles are the most aggressive form of badminton, with a high proportion of powerful jump smashes and very quick reflex exchanges. Because of this, spectator interest is sometimes greater for men's doubles than for singles.

Mixed doubles

A mixed doubles game – Scottish Schools under 12s tournament, Tranent, May 2002

In mixed doubles, both pairs typically try to maintain an attacking formation with the woman at the front and the man at the back. This is because the male players are usually substantially stronger, and can, therefore, produce smashes that are more powerful.

As a result, mixed doubles require greater tactical awareness and subtler positional play. Clever opponents will try to reverse the ideal position, by forcing the woman towards the back or the man towards the front. In order to protect against this danger, mixed players must be careful and systematic in their shot selection.

At high levels of play, the formations will generally be more flexible: the top women players are capable of playing powerfully from the back-court, and will happily do so if required. When the opportunity arises, however, the pair will switch back to the standard mixed attacking position, with the woman in front and men in the back.

ORGANIZATION

Governing bodies

The Badminton World Federation (BWF) is the internationally recognized governing body of the sport responsible for conduction of tournaments and approaching fair play. Five regional confederations are associated with the BWF:

- Asia: Badminton Asia Confederation (BAC)
- Africa: Badminton Confederation of Africa (BCA)
- Americas: Badminton Pan Am (North America and South America belong to the same confederation; BPA)
- Europe: Badminton Europe (BE)
- Oceania: Badminton Oceania (BO)

Competitions

A men's doubles match. The blue lines are those for the badminton court. The other coloured lines denote uses for other sports – such complexity being common in multi-use sports halls.

The BWF organizes several international competitions, including the Thomas Cup, the premier men's international team event first held in 1948–1949, and the Uber Cup, the women's equivalent first held in 1956–1957. The competitions now take place once every two years. More than 50 national teams compete in qualifying tournaments within continental confederations for a place in the finals. The final tournament involves 12 teams, following an increase from eight teams in 2004. It was further increased to 16 teams in 2012.

The Sudirman Cup, a gender-mixed international team event held once every two years, began in 1989. Teams are divided into seven levels based on the performance of each country.

To win the tournament, a country must perform well across all five disciplines (men's doubles and singles, women's doubles and singles, and mixed doubles). Like association football (soccer), it features a promotion and relegation system at every level. However, the system was last used in 2009 and teams competing will now be grouped by world rankings.

Badminton was a demonstration event at the 1972 and 1988 Summer Olympics. It became an official Summer Olympic sport at the Barcelona Olympics in 1992 and its gold medals now generally rate as the sport's most coveted prizes for individual players.

In the BWF World Championships, first held in 1977, currently only the highest ranked 64 players in the world, and a maximum of four from each country can participate in any category. In both the Olympic and BWF World competitions restrictions on the number of participants from any one country have caused some controversy because they sometimes result in excluding elite world level players from the strongest badminton nations. The Thomas, Uber, and Sudirman Cups, the Olympics, and the BWF World (and World Junior Championships), are all categorized as level one tournaments.

At the start of 2007, the BWF introduced a new tournament structure for the highest level tournaments aside from those in level one: the BWF Super Series. This level two tournament series, a tour for the world's elite players, stage twelve open tournaments around the world with 32 players (half the previous limit). The players collect points that determine whether they can play in Super Series Finals held at the year-end. Among the tournaments in this series is the venerable All-England Championships, first held in 1900, which was once considered the unofficial world championships of the sport.

Level three tournaments consist of Grand Prix Gold and Grand Prix event. Top players can collect the world ranking points and enable them to play in the BWF Super Series open tournaments. These include the regional competitions in Asia (Badminton Asia Championships) and Europe (European Badminton Championships), which produce the world's best players as well as the Pan America Badminton Championships.

The level four tournaments, known as International Challenge, International Series, and Future Series, encourage participation by junior players.

COMPARISON WITH TENNIS

Badminton is frequently compared to tennis. The following is a list of manifest differences:

- Scoring: In badminton, a match is played best 2 of 3 games, with each game played up to 21 points. In tennis a match is played best of 3 or 5 sets, each set consisting of 6 games and each game ends when one player wins 4 points or wins two consecutive points at deuce points. If both teams are tied at "game point", they must play until one team achieves a two-point advantage. However, at 29–all, whoever scores the golden point will win. In tennis, if the score is tied 6–6 in a set, a tiebreaker will be played, which ends once a player reaches 7 points or when one player has a two-point advantage.

- In tennis, the ball may bounce once before the point ends; in badminton, the rally ends once the shuttlecock touches the floor.

- In tennis, the serve is dominant to the extent that the server is expected to win most of his service games (at advanced level & onwards); a *break* of service, where the server loses the game, is of major importance in a match. In badminton, a server has far less an advantage and is unlikely to score an *ace* (unreturnable serve).

- In tennis, the server has two chances to hit a serve into the service box; in badminton, the server is allowed only one attempt.

- A tennis court is approximately twice the length and width of a badminton court.

- Tennis racquets are about four times as heavy as badminton racquets, 10 to 12 ounces (280 to 340 grams) versus 2 to 3 ounces (57 to 85 grams). Tennis balls are more than eleven times heavier than shuttlecocks, 57 grams (2.0 ounces) versus 5 grams (0.18 ounces).

- The fastest recorded tennis stroke is Samuel Groth's 163.4 miles per hour (263 kilometres per hour) serve, whereas the fastest badminton stroke during gameplay was Lee Chong Wei's 253 miles per hour (407 kilometres per hour) recorded smash at the 2015 Hong Kong Open.

Statistics such as the smash speed, above, prompt badminton enthusiasts to make other comparisons that are more contentious. For example, it is often claimed that badminton is the fastest racquet sport. Although badminton holds the record for the fastest initial speed of a racquet sports projectile, the shuttlecock decelerates substantially faster than other projectiles such as tennis balls. In turn, this qualification must be qualified by consideration of the distance over which the shuttlecock travels: a smashed shuttlecock travels a shorter distance than a tennis ball during a serve.

While fans of badminton and tennis often claim that their sport is the more physically demanding, such comparisons are difficult to make objectively because of the differing demands of the games. No formal study currently exists evaluating the physical condition of the players or demands during gameplay.

Badminton and tennis techniques differ substantially. The lightness of the shuttlecock and of badminton racquets allow badminton players to make use of the wrist and fingers much more than tennis players; in tennis, the wrist is normally held stable, and playing with a mobile wrist may lead to injury. For the same reasons, badminton players can generate power from a short racquet swing: for some strokes such as net kills, an elite player's swing may be less than 5 centimetres (2 inches). For strokes that require more power, a longer swing will typically be used, but the badminton racquet swing will rarely be as long as a typical tennis swing.

BADMINTON FACTS

- Badminton claims to be the second most-popular participation sport in the world. Only Soccer beats it.
- It's officially the fastest racquet sport in the world. The shuttle is smashed around the court at speeds of up to 200 mph.
- Its Olympic debut was in 1992 in Barcelona. Since 1992 Asian players have won 42 of the 46 Olympic medals.
- 1.1bn people watched the first Olympic badminton tournament on TV.
- During an average top-level match ten shuttles are used with players hitting it roughly 400 times each. It's a tiring business - they can travel several miles around the court
- The record for the shortest match? Six minutes. Ra Kyung-min (South Korea) and Julia Mann (England) hold the record. Peter Rasmussen (Denmark) and Sun Jun (China) hold the record for the longest match - 124 minutes.
- In Malaysia and Indonesia crowds of up to 15,000 people regularly fill the stands to cheer on their heroes.
- The International Badminton Federation was established in 1934 and now has 148 member countries including England, Ireland, Scotland and Wales.
- Celebrity fans include snooker player Mark Williams and

golfers Padraig Harrington and Nick Faldo. You can even buy Barbie a racquet and shuttles.

- The Chinese originally played a version of badminton called Ti Zian Ji. They didn't use racquets though, they used their feet.

- The Duke of Beaufort held parties at his estate, Badminton House in 1873. His guests were invited to play a game with shuttlecocks - and so the official game of badminton was born.

- The origin of the shuttlecock is a bit hazy. One theory is that writing feathers were stuck in corks when they weren't used. During quiet moments the 'pen' store would be thrown, or whacked, around.

- Olympic shuttles are made of 16 bird feathers, string and very strong glue. The Kansas City Museum is home to the world's largest shuttlecock - 48 times bigger than normal.

- While most players choose synthetic strings, some still use gut made from the dried stomach lining of animals such as cows or cats.

2

History of Badminton

BADMINTON FOR BEGINNERS

Badminton is becoming more and more popular and more and more students are taking up badminton as their main sport. Adults are also taking up badminton as their recreational activity in order to burn out calories and get fitter for day to day activities. As we see more beginners, I hope to point out in this article what aspects of badminton a beginner should focus on, as well as point out a few common mistakes that beginners tend to make. We hope this will help your journey into this sport that we all love. First, let's point out the positive aspects of badminton that will help the up and coming players.

Focus on the correct grip

The most fundamental aspect of badminton technique is the grip. The grip is how a badminton holds the badminton racket. A correct grip is a pathway for a badminton player to improve upon their skills. on the contrary, using an incorrect grip is often a brickwall that leads to poor form and poorly executed techniques. It takes much more time to unlearn a bad technique than to learn one. Many of us have experienced it before the painful way.

The proper badminton grips may feel uncomfortable and unnatural in the beginning, but if you are able to get over that fact, later on you will appreciate what you have learned.

There are two basic grips for badminton, the forehand grip and the backhand grip. We won't go into much more detail here, if you want to know about gripping, please read the grip guide in Badminton Central. The information maybe overwhelming at first, but since this is so fundamental in badminton, it is worth the time to digest it.

Focus on the correct strokes

The worst part of learning something is to have to unlearn it later on. This happens to many recreational badminton players. We hop into the court, invent all these wild shots that seems right then, but later on to find out that they are the wrong way to hit. Then we spend 3 times the time to unlearn them as they have been so ingrained into our muscles. If you want to avoid that happening to you, it is vital to learn the proper way in the beginning.

To do that, you must find a good coach who can direct you. When you choose a coach, make sure he understands and can demonstrate the fundamentals. Your friend who happens to be playing next court to you may not be the best coach you can get.

Focus on footwork

We cannot stress the importance of footwork more. Footwork is the skill that allows you to move from point to point in the badminton court. While it sounds like an easy concept, in fact it is one of the most difficult skills in badminton. The reason footwork is so important is very simple: if you cannot get there in time, it is useless to have the best racket skill. The Cororary of that is that, the earlier you can get to the shuttle, the more choices of shots you have and the more you can pressure your opponent.

Lee Jae Bok, an ex-Korean national player, once says:

"You hit the shuttle with your feet."

Footwork is one of the most difficult aspects of badminton. It takes a lot of time to learn, as well as a lot of time to practice.

It is often less practiced because of the lack of venue. It is quite uncommon and anti-social for someone to take up ½ of a badminton court to practice footwork while everybody waits on the sideline. Despite so, it is still very important. A professional player can move around the court very effortlessly solely because they have very good footwork technique, they do make it look very easy but in fact, it takes many years of very hard work to master it.

Focus on fitness - jog/swim/bike - or do footwork drills

Fitness is one of the many reason many people take up badminton. Depending on the level of one's game, badminton can be a very leisure game all the way to a down-right fitness torture. Beginning recreational players will likely be moving relatively less around the court, but as one's skill improve, you will not only notice that you have to cover more parts of the court, you will also have to cover it in greater speed, which multiplies the fitness level needed by many folds.

In order to catch up with your pending improvements in skill, it is then important for you to increase your fitness level to complement it. There are many ways to improve one's fitness, one popular way is to skip rope, or jog, swim, bike. Doing footwork drills also a great way to practice footwork and develop one's fitness at the same time.

Focus on keeping track of your progress

Often when one is having fun, you must try to re-evaluate what you have learned and how you are using it. Most recreational players do not do that but it is helpful in identifying potential weaknesses in your game.

Avoid expensive equipment - you will most likely be wasting money

Badminton is solely a game of skills and mind, and not a game of equipment. 99% of ones game depends on how well one can yield the racket but not depend on the racket itself.

Having said that, equipment is still one essential aspect of badminton, and one do need to get the correct equipment.

However, the most important equipment that a beginning badminton can own is not the top of the line racket, but instead a good, fitting pair of badminton shoes. Due to the nature of badminton movement, there is a high risk of injury due to twisting or spraining of various leg joints. A good pair of badminton shoes will ensure that you get a good solid grip of the badminton court and vastly reduces the risk of injury.

I'd like to mention one more thing on badminton equipment, often top of the line badminton rackets are not designed for beginners. While they are cool looking and expensive, their characteristics are more suited for advance players with more power. Beginners are best suited to lower end rackets. Your money is best suited to pay for some decent coaching instead.

Avoid trick shots - stop learning those strange shots.

Too many a time I have stepped into a badminton court against some beginning players who can do all these fancy trick shots but at the same time, unable to do a proper baseline to baseline clear. Badminton is a very fundamental game where one really need to learn all the basics in order to survive in a match. Trick shots may work once or twice but soon your opponent will learn how to read them and then you are back to square one.

There is definite a place for trick shots in badminton, but that's only after one has learned to execute all the fundamentals shots first.

Avoid fancy style - i have so many times seen beginners with really fancy looking hitting style but then they miss the shuttle completely. keep it simple.

Badminton is a very efficient game. The standard, non-fancy, way of playing badminton is the most efficient way for one to hit a shot, there is simply too little time in badminton for one to do all these fancy style.

Avoid strength training - leave this after you have learned your basic strokes.

Every now and then, someone will come to badmintoncentral and they want to know how to train their muscles to hit the strongest smash. Which is ok except we later on find out that such person cannot even hit a baseline to baseline clear properly. There is no point trying to hit hard when one cannot hit properly. An example of a proper technique is when I see 12 yrs old girls at 5 feet tall who can hit baseline to baseline clear with ease. Imagine what she can do when she grows a few inches taller?

To close, I'd like to point out that badminton is a very complex game, even advance players learn new aspects of badminton everyday. Make sure you keep an open mind when you approach badminton, only then will you be able to appreciate the greatness of this sport.

ORIGINS AND HISTORY OF BADMINTON

Facts and Information About the Game

The origins of the game of badminton date back at least 2,000 years to the game of battledore and shuttlecock played in ancient Greece, China, and India.

A very long history for one of the Olympics newest sports! Badminton took its name from Badminton House in Gloucestershire, the ancestral home of the Duke of Beaufort, where the sport was played in the last century. Gloucestershire is now the base for the International Badminton Federation.

The IBF was formed in 1934 with nine members: Canada, Denmark, France, Netherlands, England, New Zealand, Ireland, Scotland, and Wales. The United States joined four years later. Membership increased steadily over the next few years with a surge in new members after the Olympic Games debut at Barcelona.

The first big IBF tournament was the Thomas Cup (men's world team championships) in 1948. Since then, the number of world events has increased to seven, with the addition of the Uber Cup (ladies' team), World Championships, Sudirman Cup (mixed team), World Juniors, World Grand Prix Finals, and the World Cup.

The World Cup invitational event started in 1981 and is organized by the International Management Group (IMG). The World Cup series is due to end in 1997, and the IBF is considering organizing exhibition matches featuring the world's top players to replace the World Cup.

For the recent Thomas and Uber Cups in Hong Kong, the sale of commercial and television rights was a multimillion dollar contract. And it's not just in Asia. In Europe also, there's a growing number of companies bidding for rights. Television companies worldwide are already buying exclusive rights to the 1997 World Championships to be held in Glasgow, Scotland.

A turning point in badminton's growth was the $20 million tripartite contract in 1994 for sponsorship of the World Grand Prix Finals. Under the terms of the deal between the IBF, IMG, and STAR TV, STAR injects the monies into the promotion and development of badminton. In return, STAR gains total exclusivity for the exploitation of the commercial and television rights to the WGP Finals. "The deal was good for both main parties," said David Shaw, IBF's executive director, who was brought into the organization with a brief to grow the sport. "We needed a strong partner in television, and the broadcaster had identified badminton as a vehicle which would attract audiences across Asia to its prime sports channel."

The next phase in the rise and rise of international badminton has been to retake the USA. The U.S. was an early member of the IBF and initially one of the most successful. When the Uber Cup was introduced in 1956, Americans won the first three events. But then interest waned.

Badminton is a well liked and familiar sport in the USA but, predominantly, is usually played as a fun game in the backyard or on the beach. We know that once Americans see the other badminton—international badminton, the world's fastest racket sport—they will want to see and play more. The Atlanta Olympics started to raise the sport's profile in the U.S. The event was a sell-out and became one of the "must-see" sports. Ex-President Jimmy Carter, Chelsea Clinton, Paul

Newman, and Princess Anne were among the celebrities who came to watch. David Broder of the Washington Post reported "seeing one of the supreme athletic spectacles of my life."

The year 1996 was a landmark in USA badminton. It's not only the Atlanta Olympic Games that started to generate tremendous interest in the U.S. market. In December 1995, the IBF introduced a new concept tournament in California, the Hong Ta Shan Cup, a men's invitation tournament with the best players and big prize money. There are now plans to add a women's event and to increase the prize money. The Hong Ta Shan Group has gone on to sponsor the U.S. Open, increasing the prize money to $200,000. This makes the event the most valuable World Grand Prix event in the series and gives it six-star status.

The degree of change is increasing. Badminton's debut as an Olympic Games sport has manifestly boosted interest internationally. The STAR TV agreement has increased the sport's coverage dramatically.

Sponsors and television companies are being attracted to a sport which gives them access to the Asian economies. And spectators are increasingly attracted to the exciting mix of angles, tactics, touch, reaction, and fitness that would exhaust a squash champion.

HISTORY OF BADMINTON AND THE DEVELOPMENT OF THE SPORT

The history of badminton brings us all the way back to the mid-18th century.

The game of badminton started to become popular in India at a small town called *Poona*.

When India was still a British Colony badminton was played mostly by the British military officers.

At this point, Badminton was just a game played for fun, and it was known as "battledore and shuttlecock" in British India instead of Badminton.

How the Name Badminton Came About

The bat was initially referred to as "Battledore". Battledore and shuttlecock was a rather simple outdoor game.

Both players were just required to keep the shuttlecock in the air as long as possible, preventing it from touching the ground.

Battledore and shuttlecock was then brought back to England where it was introduced to the upper class community.

Eventually the game was officially introduced to the guests of the Duke of Beaufort at his house.

Interestingly, the house was called BADMINTON. The English really loved the game, and you can guess how the sport got its name "Badminton".

Historical Development of Badminton

Quick facts on the development of the sport and history of badminton:

- Official rules were developed after the game was introduced to the people in England
- The FIRST open badminton tournament was held at Guildford, England in 1898
- The FIRST All England Badminton Championships was held the following year.
- The FIRST official Badminton World Championships was held in 1977.
- Badminton became an Olympic sport in 1992.
- The Badminton World Federation (BWF) introduced the Badminton Super Series events in 2007 to further promote the sport.

Snapshot of How Badminton was played in 1960s

The video above brings you the 1964 All England Badminton Championships final.

It was played by 2 Danish players. As you can see, the

rallies were shorter. The players' movement on the court were less organized. Apart from that, the strokes were also very different compared to how we hit the shuttle nowadays.

The style of play in badminton has evolved over the years!

Technology made this possible. Rackets are lighter. Badminton shoes are better. Quality of shuttlecocks have improved.

Badminton trainings are also more intense and some are even supported by sports science.

Badminton Today

Today, badminton is considered as the FASTEST RACKET SPORT.

Badminton is played at a very intense level. Badminton players are much more athletic and agile.

The shuttlecocks are travel faster as compared to the olden days.

The video above shows you a match between the current top 2 badminton singles player in 2009, Lee Chong Wei of Malaysia and Lin Dan of China.

The match shows that players nowadays are more offensive. Their shots are also more precise.

Besides this, players also have the ability to dive and defend smashes.

Deception also became an important element in winning badminton rallies.

Strongest Badminton Nations over the Years.

England Produced the Best Player in the History of Badminton

In the early 19th century, Great Britain produced many fine players.

George Thomas was probably the BEST badminton players in the history of badminton!

He has won 21 All-England titles over his career. The largest team championships event today, the Thomas Cup Badminton Team Championships was named after George Thomas. Unfortunately we have yet to see England produce players of that class. It has been a while since the English had dominated the world of badminton.

Denmark's Dominance and their Role in the History of Badminton Denmark was the second country to produce top class badminton players.

Since the early 1900s, Denmark was a major threat in the All-England Open. That was when the All-England Open was the BIGGEST tournament before 1977.

They continued to dominate, right until today. In fact, Denmark is known very well for bringing the standard of Badminton to a higher level in the history of badminton.

Peter Gade for example showed us INSANE deceptive shots. He even produced world class badminton deception in some major competitions.

Asia Nations Dominate

Today, badminton is known to many as an "Asian sport".

This is because the Asian countries have been the most successful on the international scene. Take the biggest competition in the history of badminton (the Olympics) for example. China, Korea, Indonesia, England and Denmark were the only countries to win the Olympic Games for badminton.

Among the Asian nations, the Chinese have been winning the most titles in almost every category, including the women's category. They were so strong that they claimed TWO clean sweeps in 2010 and 2011. They took ALL 5 world champions' title in both years!

THE HISTORY OF BADMINTON

To understand the History of Badminton, first you need to understand various games that were played long before

Badminton. Let me bring you back to centuries ago where it all began...

In the 5th century BC, the people in china then played a game called ti jian zi. A direct translation from this word 'ti jian zi' is kicking the shuttle. As the name suggest, the objective of the game is to keep the shuttle from hitting the ground without using hand. Whether this sport has anything to do with the History of Badminton is up for debate. It was however the first game that uses a Shuttle.

About five centuries later, a game named Battledore and Shuttlecock was played in china, Japan, India and Greece. This is a game where you use the Battledore (a paddle) to hit the Shuttlecock back and forth. By the 16th century, it has become a popular game among children in England. In Europe this game was known as jeu de volant to them. In the 1860s, a game named Poona was played in India. This game is much like the Battledore and Shuttlecock but with an added net. The British army learned this game in India and took the equipments back to England during the 1870s.

In 1873, the Duke of Beaufort held a lawn party in his country place, Badminton. A game of Poona was played on that day and became popular among the British society's elite. The new party sport became known as "the Badminton game". In 1877, the Bath Badminton Club was formed and developed the first official set of rules.

The International Badminton Federation (IBF) was formed in 1934 with 9 founding members.

- England
- Ireland
- Scotland
- Wales
- Denmark
- Holland
- Canada

- New Zealand

- France

Since then, major international tournaments like the Thomas Cup (Men) and Uber Cup (Women) were held. Badminton was officially granted Olympic status in the 1992 Barcelona Games. From 9 founding members, IBF now have over 150 member countries. The future of Badminton looks bright indeed.

CONTEMPORARY BADMINTON

A contemporary form of badminton - a game called 'Poon', was played in India in the 1800s where a net was introduced and players hit the shuttlecock across the net. British officers in the mid 1800's took this game back to England and it was introduced as a game for the guests of the Duke of Beaufort at his stately home 'Badminton' in Gloucestershire, England where it became popular.

In March 1898, the first Open Tournament was held at Guildford the first 'All England' Championships were held the following year. Denmark, the USA and Canada became ardent followers of the game during the 1930s.

IBF Established in 1934

Then in 1934, the International Badminton Federation was formed, with the initial members including England, Wales, Ireland, Scotland, Denmark, Holland, Canada, New Zealand and France, with India joining as an affiliate in 1936.

The first major IBF tournament was the Thomas Cup (world men's team championships) in 1948. Since then, the number of world events has increased with the addition of the Uber Cup (women's team), World Championships (individual events), Sudirman Cup (mixed team), World Junior Championships and the World Grand Prix Finals.

Commonwealth Games Sport - 1966

Badminton was introduced as a Commonwealth Games

program sport in Kingston Jamaica in 1966 and has been part of every Commonwealth Games program since then. Initially all five disciplines were included – singles (men, women), doubles (men, women) and mixed doubles with the Teams Event included in the program in later Commonwealth Games.

Olympic Games Sport - 1992

Badminton is a relatively new Olympic Games sport. After being a demonstration sport in Munich in 1972, badminton became an Olympic sport in Barcelona in 1992 with the singles and doubles disciplines introduced for the first time in the Olympic Games. In Atlanta in 1996, a mixed doubles event was included and this is the only mixed doubles event in all of the Olympic sports. The following countries have won medals in badminton at an Olympic Games since its introduction in 1992 - China, Denmark, India, Indonesia, Japan, Korea, Malaysia and Russia.

Susi Susanti from Indonesia won the women's singles in Barcelona, becoming Indonesia's first medallist in the 40 years Indonesia had competed at the Games. In the same Olympic Games, Alan Budi Kusama won Indonesia's second gold medal in the men's badminton singles. : Rules of Badminton

RULES OF BADMINTON

Knowing the Rules of Badminton is important if you really want to advance in Badminton and enjoy this game. In the event that a dispute occurs during a match, you'll be able to settle it.

Toss

The rules of badminton states that a toss shall be conducted before a game starts. If you win, you can choose between serving first or to start play at either end of the court. Your opponent can then exercise the remaining choice.

Scoring system

The rules of badminton states that a badminton match

shall consist of the best of 3 games. In doubles and men's singles, the first side to score 15 points wins the game. In women's singles, the first side to score 11 points wins the game.

If the score becomes 14-all (10-all in women's singles), the side which first scored 14 (10) shall exercise the choice to continue the game to 15 (11) points or to 'set' the game to 17 (13) points.

The side winning a game serves first in the next game. Only the serving side can add a point to its score.

Recently BWF have been testing a new scoring format of 21 points per game on all major Badminton competition and decided to replace the old format permanently.

Change of ends

The rules of badminton states that you have to change ends with your opponent after finishing the first game. If a third game was to be played, you shall change ends when the leading score reaches 6 in a game of 11 points or 8 in a game of 15 points.

Rules of Badminton - Singles

Serving and receiving courts

You shall serve from, and receive in, the right service court when you or your opponent has scored an even number of points in that game.

You shall serve from, and receive in, the left service court when you or your opponent has scored an odd number of points in that game.

You and your opponent will hit the shuttle alternately until a 'fault' is made or the shuttle ceases to be in play.

Scoring and serving

You score a point and serve again from the alternate service court when your opponent makes a 'fault' or the shuttle ceases to be in play because it touches the surface of your opponent's side of court. No points will be scored when you make a 'fault' or the shuttles ceases to be in play because it touches the surface of your side of court. The serving right will then be transferred to your opponent.

Rules of Badminton - Doubles

At the start of the game, and each time a side gains the right to serve, the service shall be delivered from the right service court. Only your opponent standing diagonally opposite of you shall return the service.

Should your opponent's partner touched or hit the shuttle, it shall be a 'fault' and your side scores a point.

Order of play and position on court

After the service is returned, either you or your partner may hit the shuttle from any position on your side of the net. Then either player from the opposing side may do the same, and so on, until the shuttle ceases to be in play.

Scoring and serving

If you are serving or receiving first at the start of any game, you shall serve or receive in the right service court when your side or your opponent's side scored an even number of points.

You shall serve from or receive in the left service court when your side or your opponent's side has scored an odd number of points. The reverse pattern shall apply to your partner. In any game, the right to serve passes consecutively from the initial server to the initial receiver, then to that initial's receiver's partner, then to the opponent who is due to serve from the right service court, then to that player's partner, and so on. You shall not serve out of turn, receive out of turn, or receive two consecutive services in the same game, except as provided in service court errors and 'lets'.

Service court errors

A service court error has been made when a player has served out of turn, has served from the wrong service or standing on the wrong service court while being prepared to receive the service and it has been delivered.

If a service court error is discovered after the next service had been delivered, the error shall not be corrected. If a service court error is discovered before the next service is delivered, the following rules apply.

If both sides committed an error, it shall be a 'let'. If one side committed the error and won the rally, it shall be a 'let'. If one side committed the error and lost the rally, the error shall not be corrected.

If there is a 'let' because of a service court error, the rally is replayed with the error corrected. If a service court error is not to be corrected, play in that game shall proceed without changing the player's new service courts.

Faults

The rules of badminton consider the following as faults:

- If the shuttle lands outside the boundaries of the court, passes through or under the net, fail to pass the net, touches the ceiling or side walls, touches the person or dress of a player or touches any other object or person.

- If the initial point of contact with the shuttle is not on the striker's side of the net. (The striker may, however, follow the shuttle over the net with the racket in the course of a stroke.)

- If a player touches the net or its supports with racket, person or dress, invades an opponent's court over the net with racket or person except as permitted.

- If a player invades an opponent's court under the net with racket or person such that an opponent is obstructed or distracted or obstructs an opponent, that is prevents an opponent from making a legal stroke where the shuttle is followed over the net.

- If a player deliberately distracts an opponent by any action such as shouting or making gestures.

- If the shuttle is caught and held on the racket and then slung during the execution of a stroke.
- If the shuttle is hit twice in succession by the same player with two strokes.
- If the shuttle is hit by a player and the player's partner successively or touches a player's racket and continues towards the back of that player's court.
- If a player is guilty of flagrant, repeated or persistent offences under Law of Continuous Play, Misconduct, Penalties.
- If, on service, the shuttle is caught on the net and remains suspended on top, or, on service, after passing over the net is caught in the net.

Lets

'Let' is called by the umpire, or by a player (if there is no umpire), to halt play.

A 'let' may be given for any unforeseen or accidental occurrence.The rules of badminton consider the following as 'lets':

- If a shuttle is caught in the net and remains suspended on top or, after passing over the net, is caught in the net, it shall be a 'let' except on service.
- If, during service, the receiver and server are both faulted at the same time, it shall be a 'let'.
- If the server serves before the receiver is ready, it shall be a 'let'.
- If, during play, the shuttle disintegrates and the base completely separates from the rest of the shuttle, is shall be a 'let'.
- If a line judge is unsighted and the umpire is unable to make a decision, it shall be a 'let'.
- A 'let' may occur following a service court error. When a 'let' occurs, the play since the last service shall not count and the player who served shall serve again, except where

in situations where the Law of Service Court Errors is applicable.

Shuttle not in play

A shuttle is not in play when it strikes the net and remains attached there or suspended on top.

A shuttle is not in play when it strikes the net or post and starts to fall towards the surface of the court on the striker's side of the net.

A shuttle is not in play when it hits the surface of the court or a 'fault' or 'let' has occurred.

Continuous play, misconduct, penalties

Play shall be continuous from the first service until the match is concluded, except as allowed in intervals not exceeding 90 seconds between the first and second games, and not exceeding 5 minutes between the second and third games.

Officials and appeals

The referee is in overall charge of the tournament. The umpire, where appointed, is in charge of the match, the court and its immediate surrounds. The umpire shall report to the referee. The service judge shall call service faults made by the server should they occur. A line judge shall indicate whether a shuttle landed 'in' or 'out' on the line or lines assigned. An official's decision is final on all points of fact for which that official is responsible.

SIMPLE RULES FOR COMPLETE BEGINNERS

The absolute basics

The aim of badminton is to hit the shuttle with your racket so that it passes over the net and lands inside your opponent's half of the court. Whenever you do this, you have won a rally; win enough rallies, and you win the match.

Your opponent has the same goal. He will try to reach the shuttle and send it back into your half of the court. You can also win rallies from your opponent's mistakes: if he hits the shuttle into or under the net, or out of court, then you win the rally.

If you think your opponent's shot is going to land *out*, then you should let it fall to the floor. If you hit the shuttle instead, then the rally continues.

Once the shuttle touches the ground, the rally is over. In this respect, badminton is not like tennis or squash, where the ball can bounce.

You must hit the shuttle once only before it goes over the net (even in doubles). In this respect, badminton is not like volleyball, where multiple players can touch the ball before sending it back over the net.

Badminton is played indoors

Some of you may be familiar with playing badminton on a beach, or in the garden. This is fine when you're playing it as a casual game, but it doesn't work when you start to get competitive.

The shuttle is blown off course by even the slightest breath of wind. That's why competitive badminton is always played indoors.

Setting up a badminton court

Badminton has its own nets and posts; the net is much lower than for volleyball. Sometimes a sports centre will set up the court with a slack volleyball net instead, because the staff don't know anything about badminton. Ask for proper badminton posts and a badminton net.

If you need to set up the court yourself, then check three things:

- The net covers the whole width of the court.
- The net is pulled tight, not slack.
- The net is in the middle, so that both court halves are the same size.

Often it can be hard to see the badminton court lines, because lines for other sports are also painted on the floor. The badminton court lines should all be in one colour, so try to focus on that.

Singles, doubles, and mixed doubles

You can have either two or four players on a badminton court: one player on each side, or a team of two players on each side. One-against-one is called singles; two-against-two is called doubles.

In doubles, either player can hit the shuttle; you do not have to take it in turns. The only exceptions are the first two shots of the rally; I'll explain this when we discuss *serving*.

In total, there are five types of badminton:

- Men's singles
- Women's singles
- Men's doubles
- Women's doubles
- Mixed doubles (each team is a man and a woman)

Men's doubles and women's doubles are also called *level* doubles.

These are the only types of badminton played in serious tournaments. In casual play, however, women sometimes play against men (e.g. two women against two men).

What are all those lines for?

When you first look at a badminton court, you could be forgiven for thinking it has too many lines. This is mainly because the court is marked up for both singles and doubles, which use slightly different court sizes.

The outermost lines form the doubles court. So in a doubles rally, the shuttle is allowed to land anywhere on the court.

The singles court is slightly narrower than the doubles court. The singles side lines are not the outermost lines, but the next ones in. Taken together with the outermost (doubles) side lines, these make narrow alley shapes along the sides of the court. These alleys are often called the *tramlines* or *side tramlines*, since they look like tram or train tracks.

So here's another way to think about it: the side tramlines are *in* for doubles, but *out* for singles.

All the other lines are for serving

There are still three lines we haven't discussed yet. These lines mean nothing during the main rally, and only apply when you're serving. This is similar to how a tennis court has special lines for serving.

Serving

Serving is how you start the rally: someone has to hit the shuttle first! To prevent the server gaining an overwhelming advantage, there are special restrictions placed on serving that don't apply during the rest of the rally.

The *receiver* is the person who hits the second shot in the rally. In doubles, the receiver's partner is not allowed to hit this shot.

How to serve

In badminton, the serve must be hit in an upwards direction, with an underarm hitting action. You are not allowed to play a tennis style serve.

The main rule here is that when you hit the shuttle, it must be below your waist. To be exact, the rules define this to be a height level with the lowest part of your ribcage. In other words, you can serve from a bit higher than the top of your shorts, but not much.

Service courts

The service courts are smaller box shapes inside the court. We'll look at what they are used for in a moment, but first let's get the right boxes.

Notice that the badminton court has a line down the middle, extending from the back to near the net; this is the *centre line*. At the front of the court, the centre line is met by another line; this is the front service line. These two lines form a T shape where they meet.

A singles service court is a box made from four lines:

- The centre line
- A singles side line (inside side line)
- The front service line
- The back line (the outside one, all the way at the back)

On your side of the net, you have two service courts: your right service court, and your left service court. The same is true for your opponent.

The doubles service courts are slightly different. They are wider, because they use the outside side line (remember: the doubles court is wider); and they are shorter, because they use the inside back line.

That's what the inside back line is for: doubles service, and nothing else. It's probably the most confusing line on a badminton court, because that's all it does!

So just to be clear, a doubles service court is made from these four lines:

- The centre line
- A doubles side line (outside side line)
- The front service line
- The inside back line (not the very back line, but the next one in)

How service courts are used

Service courts are used for three things:

- The server must stand inside a service court.
- The receiver must stand inside the diagonally opposite service court.

- The serve must travel into the diagonally opposite service court.

For example, suppose the server is standing in his left service court. The receiver will be standing in *his* left service court, which is also where the serve has to go.

If the serve is going to land outside the service court, then the receiver should let it fall to the floor. If the receiver hits the serve, then the rally continues even if the serve had been going *out*.

The server and receiver must stay inside their service boxes until the server contacts the shuttle with his racket. After that, they can leave the boxes immediately and move anywhere on court.

3

Badminton Rules and Regulations

Badminton is a sport that has been around since the 16th century. The sport is played indoors and the pinnacle comes from its Olympic events. The sport is very popular in Asian countries such as China and India with these countries leading the way by producing some of the world's best players.

Object of the Game

The object of badminton is to hit the shuttlecock over the net and have it land in the designated court areas. If your opponent manages to return the shuttlecock then a rally occurs. If you win this rally i.e. force your opponent to hit the shuttlecock out or into the net then you win a point. You are required to win 21 points to win a set with most matches being best of 3 sets. Points can be won on either serve.

Players & Equipment

There are two forms of badminton, singles and doubles (it's also possible to play mixed doubles). Each player is allowed to use a stringed racket (similar to a tennis racket but with the head being smaller) and a shuttlecock. The shuttlecock is made up of half round ball at the bottom and a feather like material surrounding the top. You can only really hit the bottom of the shuttlecock and as gravity comes into play will always revert the ball side facing down. You may only hit the shuttlecock once before it either hits the ground or goes over the net.

The court measures 6.1m wide and 13.4m long. Across the middle of the rectangular court is a net which runs at 1.55m. Running along each side of the court are two tram lines. The inside lines are used as the parameter for singles match whilst the outside line is used for a doubles match.

Scoring

A point is scored when you successfully hit the shuttlecock over the net and land it in your opponent's court before they hit it. A point can also be gained when your opponent hits the shuttlecock into either the net or outside the parameters.

Winning the Game

To win a game you must reach 21 points before your opponent. If you do so then you will have won that set. If the scores are tied at 20-20 then it comes down to whichever player manages to get two clear points ahead. If the points are still tied at 29-29 then the next point will decide the winner of the set. Winning the overall game will require you to win 2 out of the 3 sets played.

Rules of Badminton

- A game can take place with either two (singles) or four (doubles) players.

- An official match has to be played indoors on the proper court dimensions. The dimensions are 6.1m by 13.4m, The net is situated through the middle of the court and is set at 1.55m.

- To score a point the shuttlecock must hit within the parameters of the opponents court.

- If the shuttlecock hits the net or lands out then a point is awarded to your opponent.

- Players must serve diagonally across the net to their opponent. As points are won then serving stations move from one side to the other. There are no second serves so if your first serve goes out then your opponent wins the point.

- A serve must be hit underarm and below the servers waist. No overarm serves are allowed.

- Each game will start with a toss to determine which player will serve first and which side of the court the opponent would like to start from.

- Once the shuttlecock is 'live' then a player may move around the court as they wish. They are permitted to hit the shuttlecock from out of the playing area.

- If a player touches the net with any part of their body or racket then it is deemed a fault and their opponent receives the point.

- A fault is also called if a player deliberately distracts their opponent, the shuttlecock is caught in the racket then flung, the shuttlecock is hit twice or if the player continues to infract with the laws of badminton.

- Each game is umpired by a referee on a high chair who overlooks the game. There are also line judges who monitor if the shuttlecock lands in or not. The referee has overriding calls on infringements and faults.

- Let may be called by the referee if an unforeseen or accidental circumstance arose. These may include the shuttlecock getting stuck in the bet, server serving out of turn, one player was not ready or a decision which is too close to call.

- The game has only two rest periods coming the form of a 90 second rest after the first game and a 5 minute rest period after the second game.
- If the laws are continuously broken by a player then the referee holds the power to dock that player of points with persisting fouls receiving a forfeit of the set or even the match.

SIMPLIFIED RULES

Scoring System

  o A match consists of the best of 3 games of 21 points.
  o Every time there is a serve – there is a point scored.
  o The side winning a rally adds a point to its score.
  o At 20 all, the side which gains a 2 point lead first, wins that game.
  o At 29 all, the side scoring the 30th point, wins that game.
  o The side winning a game serves first in the next game.

Interval and Change of Ends

  o When the leading score reaches 11 points, players have a 60 second interval.
  o A 2 minute interval between each game is allowed.
  o In the third game, players change ends when the leading score reaches 11 points.

Singles

  o At the beginning of the game (0-0) and when the server's score is even, the server serves from the right service court. When the server's score is odd, the server serves from the left service court.
  o If the server wins a rally, the server scores a point and then serves again from the alternate service court.

o If the receiver wins a rally, the receiver scores a point and becomes the new server. They serve from the appropriate service court – left if their score is odd, and right if it is even.

Doubles

o A side has only one 'set'.

o The service passes consecutively to the players as shown in the diagram.

o At the beginning of the game and when the score is even, the server serves from the right service court. When it is odd, the server serves from the left court.

o If the serving side wins a rally, the serving side scores a point and the same server serves again from the alternate service court.

o If the receiving side wins a rally, the receiving side scores a point. The receiving side becomes the new serving side.

o The players do not change their respective service courts until they win a point when their side is serving.

BADMINTON RULES (DOUBLES AND SINGLES)

All games are played to 21 points — win by 2!

Rally Scoring is the official scoring for badminton!

Scoring System

• A match consists of single game of 21 points.

• Every time there is a serve – there is a point scored.

• The side winning a rally adds a point to its score.

Doubles

(follow rules for "Scoring System")

1. Each side has only one "set" – only one partner has a chance to score points.

2. At the beginning of the game and when the score is even,

the server serves from the right service court. When it is odd, the server serves from the left court.

- If the serving side wins a rally, the serving side scores a point and the same server serves again from the alternate service court.

- If the receiving side wins a rally, the receiving side scores a point. The receiving side becomes the new serving side.

- The players do not change their respective service courts until they win a point when their side is serving.

Singles

(follow rules for "Scoring System")

1. At the beginning of the game and when the score is even, the server serves from the right service court. When it is odd, the server serves from the left court.

2. If the receiving side wins a rally, the receiving side scores a point. The receiving side becomes the new serving side.

3. The players do not change their respective service courts until they win a point when their side is serving.

Hits/Etiquette

1. All serves must be *below the waist,* and the racket head must be *below the wrist* — NO OVERHEAD SERVES!!!

2. To determine the serve at the beginning of the game, flip the birdie. Whoever it points to may choose serve or side. If they choose to serve or not to serve, their opponent may choose the preferred side and vice versa.

3. Please go over lines before the game begins so that both you and your opponent are familiar with the differences between serving lines in doubles and singles.

4. Have fun!

DOUBLE'S RULES FOR BADMINT ON

Doubles badminton is played with four players, or two on

each side of the net. Unlike singles badminton, the boundaries of a doubles game are marked by the outer lines of the court. The one exception to this rule is that the server uses the inner back line. The net on a doubles badminton court is set at 5 feet high. Rules for doubles badminton play are set by the International Badminton Federation.

Service

Before each doubles match begins, service is determined by the flip of a coin. The International Badminton Federation, or IBF, states that service for doubles always takes place in the right service court. The team that serves is known as the server and the other team is known as the receiver. The receiver in the court that is diagonally across from the server, must return the shuttle.

After the initial serve is returned, play continues with any player hitting the shuttle from any court. Serving alternates between the right and left courts as long as the initial server wins points, according to the Iowa State University Recreation Services. Once the serving team loses a point, the serve is won by the other team. When the first team wins the serve again, the second player on the first team now serves.

General Play

After the serve has been returned, either doubles partner can return the shuttle from any position on the badminton court, according to the IBF. Shuttles that land on the boundary lines are considered inbounds. The shuttle is considered "good" and play is continued even when it touches the net but still passes over to the other side. Shuttles that touch the ground in between plays are faults and can cause the serving team to win points. Each doubles team—but only one player per team— can only hit the shuttle once before it passes over the net.

Scoring

Badminton doubles games are played until one team wins the game with 11 points. The serving team can win points; the other team must wait until they win the serve in order to score. Unlike some other racket sports, gaining a two-point lead in order to win the game is not necessary in doubles badminton.

RULES OF BADMINTON & SCORING

As with any sport it is important to know the rules of badminton. After all, you wouldn't want your opponent gaining an unfair advantage over you just because you aren't sure about them! It is also worth noting that the rules have been changed in recent years in an attempt to make the game more exciting and entertaining to watch. The laws of badminton are highly complex and technical, but here is a brief overview of the key points to know:

Badminton scoring system

The scoring system for badminton has changed in recent years. This was done to speed games up and make them more entertaining to watch. A badminton game is now played up to 21 points, and a point can be scored from every rally, irregardless of who is serving. Under the old system a point could only be scored by the player holding the serve. If the score reaches 20-20 then a two-point advantage is required for victory, however. If no player has managed to achieve this two-point advantage by the time the score reaches 29-29, then the first player to reach 30 is the winner. Matches are generally played over the best-of-three sets.

Serving

The rules regarding the serve in badminton are very particular. Here are the key points to remember:

Singles

- At the beginning of the game (0-0) and when the servers score is even, the server serves from the right service court. When the server's score is odd, the server serves from the left service court.
- If the server wins a rally, the server scores a point and then serves again from the alternate service court.
- If the receiver wins a rally, the receiver scores a point and becomes the new server. They serve from the appropriate service court; left if their score is odd, and right if it is even.

Doubles

- Each pair only has one serve.
- At the beginning of the game and when the score is even, the server serves from the right service court. When it is odd, the server serves from the left court.
- If the serving side wins a rally, the serving side scores a point and the same server serves again from the alternate service court.
- If the receiving side wins a rally, the receiving side scores a point. The receiving side becomes the new serving side.
- The players do not change their respective service courts until they win a point when their side is serving.

Another key rule regarding the serve in badminton is that the point of impact between racket and shuttlecock must be below the players waist. The shaft of the racket must also be angled in a downward direction. So, the serve in badminton should always be an underarm shot!

For help with serving, see our tips here! Is that 'in' or 'out'? Whether a particular shot is deemed 'in' or 'out' will differ depending if you are playing singles or doubles.

BADMINTON RULES

Singles and Doubles

The Game

1. Participants are subject to all policies and procedures in the Intramural Handbook.

2. The game is played by two players in singles and four players in doubles.

3. Match Scoring: Best 2 out of 3 games will decide the winner of the match.

4. Game Time: 45 minute time limit. If the time limit expires during the final game of the match, the score at that time will determine the winner. If the game is tied or only one point separates the opponents, the first player ahead by two points will be awarded the game and match.

5. Rest Period between Games: A two-minute rest period is allowed between game one and two. Players are not permitted to leave the court. A 5-minute rest period is allowed between the second and third game during which time players are allowed to leave the court.

6. Rights and Duties of Participants: The participants are responsible for officiating their own match. Any call that can not be agreed on must be replayed.

Serving

1. Badminton serves must be executed underhand and below the waist. The shuttle must be contacted below the waistline, and the racket head must be completely below the handle. However, the racket handle may be above the waist.

2. Neither server nor receiver may move either of his/her feet from the court until the shuttle is contacted.

3. A service that tips the net and falls into the proper court is a legal serve.

4. A serve may not be executed until the receiver indicated that he/she is ready.

5. Singles Serving

   1. The initial serve for either player in singles must be executed from the right-hand service court to the opposite right-hand service court.

   2. If a point is scored, the serve should be attempted from the left-hand service court to the opposite left-hand service court.

   3. After each point is scored, the players must alternate sides.

   4. If a point is not scored by the server, a "side-out" is called. The opponent then has a "side-in" and commences to serve.

   5. When an opponent is defeated in their attempts to serve, the side-in player must go back to the side of the court in which they last served.

   6. If the server's score is an odd number, for example, 1,3,5, the next service will be from the left service court.

   7. When the server has an even number score, for example, 0,2,4, the next serve must be executed from the right court.

6. Doubles Serving

   1. The initial serve by either team in doubles must be executed from the right-hand court.

   2. The serving team alternates serving courts after each point is scored. however, the receiving team members must remain in their same service courts even though their opponents are switching service courts.

   3. Only the proper player may return a serve without forfeiting the point.

Scoring

1. All games are played to 15 points.

2. A match consists of the best two out of three games.

3. Sides change courts at the end of each game; the winning side serves first in the following game.

4. If a third game is necessary, players change ends of the court when either side first reaches eight in a game of 15 points.

5. There is no "setting" in Intramural Badminton all games must be won by 2 points or first to 21.

Playing Regulations:

1. If the server completely misses the shuttle on a serve, he/she may re-stroke. An infinite number of attempts may be made, provided the racket does not touch any part of the shuttle.

2. The shuttle is still in play if a player completely misses the shuttle on an attempted hit.

3. A shuttle falling on the boundary line is considered good.

4. A serve or a shot during a rally or exchange, which touches the net, is considered good as long as it falls within the proper boundaries.

5. A let (replay of the point) is called when any unusual occurrence interferes with the play.

Faults

1. If on the serve, the shuttle is contacted above the server's waist.

2. If during the serve, the feet of server and receiver are not within boundaries of their respective service courts.

3. If in serving, the shuttle lands outside the boundaries of the service court (i.e., into the one not diagonally opposite to the server).

4. If either in service or play, the shuttle falls outside the boundaries of the court, or passes through or under the

net, or fails to pass the net, or touches the roof or side walls, or the person or clothing of a player.

5. If the shuttle in play be struck before it crosses to the striker's side of the net. The striker may, however, follow the shuttle over the net with the racket in the course of his stroke.

6. If when the shuttle is in play a player touches the net of its supports with racket, person, or clothing.

7. If the shuttle is held on the racket while struck (i.e., be caught or slung).

8. It is not a fault if the frame, shaft, or handle of the racket hits the shuttle, or if the base and the feathers of the shuttle are struck simultaneously.

RULES AND REGULATIONS

Doubles and Singles

Badminton can be played by two or four players. In a singles, two single players (two men or two women) play against each other. A doubles consists of two opposing pairs of players. There are ladies' doubles (two pairs of ladies playing against each other), men's doubles (two pairs of two men playing against each other) and mixed doubles (two pairs consisting of one man and one woman playing against each other). The game therefore has five disciplines: ladies' singles, ladies' doubles, men's singles, men's doubles, and mixed doubles.

The Court

In normal play, the court is 13.40m long and 5.10m (singles) or 6.10m (doubles) wide. The height of the net is 1.524m over the centre of the court, but 1.55m over the side lines of the doubles court.

The singles court always covers the full length of the court, from base line to base line, both in normal play and for the service. Similarly, singles are always played on the narrow court.

Doubles are always played on the wide court. During a rally, the base line at the back of the court marks the end of the court. However, a doubles service must be played into the short service court, marked by the doubles service line 80 centimetres before the base line.

The Toss

At the beginning of each match, a toss is made to determine which side serves first. The winner of the toss can chose whether to make the first service of the match or whether to return first, thus leaving the first service to the opponent. The side that lost the toss can then chose on which end of the court he/she/they want to start.

Alternatively, the side that wins the toss may also choose to select the end of the curt on which he/she/they want(s) to start. The right to decide who makes the first service in the match then goes to the side that lost the toss.

The Sets

A badminton match commonly consists of up to three sets. The side that first reaches 21 points wins a set (exception: when there is no two-point difference). The side that first wins two sets wins the match. A third set is played if, after two sets, both sides have won one each.

After each set, the sides change ends. A short break of up to 90 seconds can be made between sets and in the middle of each set, when the first player reaches 11 points. Strictly speaking, the players may not leave the court during the break, but coaching is allowed.

Scoring

A rally is won by one side if it plays the shuttle in such a way that it cannot be returned by the opponents and hits the ground inside the opponent's court (including on the lines), if the opponent's return does not cross the net or if the opponent's return hits the ground outside the court boundaries. Furthermore, a side wins the rally if:

- (one of) the opposing player(s) touches the shuttle with the body before it hits the ground (whether inside or outside the court)
- (one of) the opposing player(s) touches the net with the racket or the body while the shuttle is in the air
- (one of) the opposing player(s) hits the shuttle before it has crossed the net (i.e. reaching over to the opponent's side of the court)
- both players of one side in a doubles touch the shuttle
- one player touches the shuttle more than once
- a faulty service is played

The basic scoring rules are:

- The winner of each rally scores a point, regardless of who is serving. This means that every mistake, even a faulty service, wins the opponent a point. (Avoidable) mistakes are thus penalised quite heavily.
- The player winning a rally scores a point and simultaneously wins (or keeps) the right to serve.
- The winning score in each set is 21 points, but to win a set, a side must lead their opponents by two points or more.
- A player must lead his/her opponents by a minimum of two points in order to win a set. The closest possible winning score with 21 points is therefore 21-19. If the score reaches 20-20, the set is won by the first player or pair building up a two point lead or by the first player or pair to score 30 points. This means that possible winning scores are 22-20, 21-23, 22-24,..., 29-27, 30-28 - or 30-29: if score reaches 29-29, the next player to score a point wins the set with a score of 30-29. This is the only exception when no margin of two points is needed to win a set.
- The winning score for a set is the same in all five disciplines.
- Even in a doubles, each side only has one service. As in the singles disciplines, the service is played from the left

or the right service court, depending on whether the score of the serving side is odd or even. The service is always played from the left service court if the serving side's score is odd or from the right service court if it is even. In doubles, players of the serving side change service courts with every point they score, but if a side scores a point without having served, they do not change service courts.

Serving

Every service, in singles and doubles, must be played across the front service line, nearly 2 metres away from the net, and always into the diagonally opposite service court. Each side has one service (in singles and in doubles). If the serving side's score is even, the service must be played from the right service court, if it is odd, from the left service court. The first service (at 0-0) is always played from the right service court.

If the serving side scores a point, it keeps the service and starts the next rally with a new service from the left or right service court, depending on whether its score is odd or even. If the returning side scores a point, it also wins the right to serve. This principle applied to singles as well as to doubles matches.

In singles, the position of the serving player is easy to ascertain as it always and only depends on whether the serving player's score is odd (left service court) or even (right service court).

In doubles, a little more care needs to be taken as the two players of a side take it in turns to serve. Again, the service court from which the service is played depends on whether the score is odd (left) or even (right). If the side of the serving player scores a point, the player keeps the right to serve and moves to the other service court for the next service. This procedure continues until the returning side wins a point. In this case, they also win the right to serve, but they do not change service courts at that point. Service courts are only changed by the serving side.

Example: A and B play against C and D. A and C start the set on their respective right service courts, B and D on the left service courts. At 0-0, A plays the first service from the right service court. C is the returning player. If A and B win the rally, they score a point and lead 1-0. A then moves to the left service court (and B, by implication, to the right one). C and D remain where they are. At 1-0, A serves again, this time from the left. C and D win the rally and score a point. However, as they did not serve in this rally, they do not change service courts. At a score of 1-1, their score is odd and therefore D, being the player on the left service court, wins the right to serve. D then serves to A and C and D win another point. They therefore change service courts and D continues to serve, this time from the right hand side, at a score of 2-1. If A and B win the next rally, they equalise and win back the right to serve without changing service courts. A is now on the left service court and the side's score is even (2-2), therefore B wins the right to serve (from the right service court).

SIMPLIFIED BADMINTON RULES AND REGULATIONS

Badminton is one of the most popular racquet sports in Singapore. Equipments are relatively inexpensive which makes it easy for new players to take up the sport. To get started, all you need is a badminton court, net, racquets and shuttlecocks.

Badminton is fun which makes it a good activity for family and friends to bond. At the same time, it is also an effective calorie-burner that not only builds strength but put your reflexes to the test. After all, players are required to run, lunge, stretch, leap and jump around the 20 x 44 feet rectangular court.

The coin toss – who goes first?

Before a tournament starts, a coin is tossed. The winner of the coin toss will then get to choose either

1) to serve or to receive or

2) the preferred side of the court.

The loser of the coin toss will then exercise the remaining choice.

Service

A serve is delivered diagonally across the courts. During service, both the server and receiver must stand at diagonally opposite sides without touching the boundary lines of the badminton courts. During a serve, the point at which the racquet is allowed to come into contact with the shuttlecock must happen below the server's waist.

Rally

A rally starts with a serve, often times continuing with a series of shots exchanged between opposing sides before it finally ends when a point is scored.

Badminton Scoring System – 3 (games) x 21 (points)

The 3 (game sets) x 21 (points) scoring system was first introduced in December 2005 and is now the official scoring system used at professional tournaments. Despite the official updates to the rules, some recreational players (particularly those who have been playing badminton for many years) still follow the traditional scoring system.

A badminton match consists of three games.

The first player/team to score 21 points wins a game.

A point is awarded to the player/team that wins the rally.

In the event that a game reaches a 20-20 score, players can only win the set by getting a 2 point lead over the opposing party e.g. 22-20, 23-21, 24-22 etc.

In the event that the game reaches a 29-29 score, the first team to reach 30 points will win the set and take the service for the next game.

Switching sides on the court

Players/teams will switch sides on the court

At the end of the first game

At the end of the second game if there is a third game

During the third game the first player/team scores 11 points.

RULES AND REGULATIONS FOR BADMINT ON SINGLES

Scoring System for Badminton Singles

1. Badminton Singles is a match consists of the best of 3 games of 21 points.
2. Every time there is a serve – there is a point scored.
3. The side winning a rally adds a point to its score.
4. At 20 all, the side which gains a 2 point lead first, wins that game.
5. At 29 all, the side scoring the 30th point, wins that game.
6. The side winning a game serves first in the next game.

Rules and Regulations for Badminon Singles

1. At the beginning of the game (0-0) and when the server's score is even, the server serves from the right service court.

When the server's score is odd, the server serves from the left service court.

2. If the server wins a rally, the server scores a point and then serves again from the alternate service court.

3. If the receiver wins a rally, the receiver scores a point and becomes the new server. They serve from the appropriate service court – left if their score is odd, and right if it is even.

THE NEW BADMINTON RULES

In August 2006, the Badminton World Federation, or BWF, changed the laws of badminton in order to add extra excitement to the game. The rule changes were designed to regulate the duration of each match and make the sport more appealing for television audiences. All court measurements and equipment laws have remained unchanged, as have the basic playing methods. The main changes have been to the scoring system.

Game Length

As with the former rules of badminton, you have to win two out of three games to win a match. However, the traditional

15 points format has now been replaced with a 21 points format. Before the rule changes, each game would be won by the first player to score 15 points, or 11 points for women. The new rules state that the first player to score 21 points will win each game. This rule applies for both men and women.

Scoring

The new scoring system has not lengthened the duration of each match. Due to the new points system, the game now flows more rapidly. Points used to be won only on the serve, meaning that the receiving player had to break his opponent's serve in order to win the right to serve and therefore score points. The new rules have introduced what is known as a "rally scoring system." A player or team can now win a point in any rally, regardless of who served.

Tied Games

The 21 point format has also brought in new laws for tied games. According to the official Badminton World Federation Laws of Badminton, "If the score becomes 20-all, the side which gains a two point lead first, shall win that game." If the score becomes 29-all, the player or team to score the 30th point will win the game.

Break

Due to changes in the points scoring system, players now receive a 60-second break when one side reaches 11 points. All players get a two-minute break between each game.

Doubles

All of the new rules also apply to doubles matches. An additional change has been introduced into the doubles serving system. As stated by the BBC Sport website, "A team now has only one serve in doubles, rather than two under the old rules."

Overall Difference

The new badminton rules have reduced the playing time

needed to complete a full match. According to the Badminton Information website, it was not uncommon for an old format match to last for two hours. The new rules have reduced the average match time to about an hour. The rally scoring system has also changed the tactical nature of the game. As the Badminton Information website states, "Avoiding making unforced errors is crucial here because every rally counts."

BADMINTON RULES (RULES AND REGULATIONS OF BADMINT ON)

Badminton is the fastest racket sport in the world. In order to develop your skills and to enjoy the game, you must be aware of its rules and regulations. The rules for singles and doubles vary. These rules are made by BWF (Badminton World Federation) . BWF is the governing body of badminton. All of the Badminton Rules (Rules and Regulations of Badminton) as determined by the Badminton world federation are explained below.

The object of the game

The basic object of the game is to hit the shuttle with your racket so that it may pass over the net and land in your opponent's half of the court. You must hit the shuttle only once (this applies for both singles and doubles). Your opponent also has the same goal, to hit the shuttle over the net so that it lands on your side of the court.

When the shuttle has touched the ground, the rally is over. Badminton is not like tennis or squash. You must win the rallies to gain points. You also win rallies when your opponent faults, for example if he hits the shuttle outside the court, or the shuttle fails to pass over the net. So if you think that the shuttle is going to land outside of the court then you should let it fall, if you hit it instead then the rally will continue.

Some of you may have played or seen other people playing badminton on beaches and other outdoor places, that's fine if you want to play it as a casual game. But if you want to be competitive and want to improve your game and play on higher levels then you must play the game indoors because the shuttle's flight is affected by the slightest wind disturbances.

Scoring System

- A match consists of three games.
- Each game consists of 21 points.
- At 20 all, the side that scores 2 consecutive points will win .
- If the scores ties at 29 all, then the side that scores the 30th point will win the game.
- The side winning the game gets to serve first in the next game.

Intervals during the game

- An interval of 60 seconds is given when a side has scored 11 points (this applies for both singles and doubles).
- When the game ends, an interval of 2 minutes is allowed before starting the next game.

Change of endscourts

- Sidescourts are changed after the game has ended (for the first two games).

- During the third game the sides are changed when the leading score reaches 11.

Toss

A toss is made before the start of a match. The side that wins the toss chooses either between serving first or the side of the court.

Serving

- The serve is done diagonally in badminton.
- The point of contact of the shuttle with the racket must be below the waist line of the player that is serving.
- The shuttle must land within the receiver's court.

Serving rotation in Singles

- At love all (0 – 0) when the score of both the players is even, the player will serve from the right side of the court.
- When the score is odd, the player will serve from the left side of the court.
- If a server wins a rally a point will be added to his score and he will serve from the alternative court.
- If the receiver wins a rally he will gain a point and become the new server. If his points are even then he will serve from the right and if his points are odd the he will serve from the left.

Serving rotation in Doubles

Serving in doubles is a tiny bit complex than serving in singles, but the basic concept is the same. BWF has explained them in an amazing way so that everyone can understand them easily.

LAWS OF BADMINTON

The game

Like tennis, badminton can be played by singles and doubles, mixed or same sex. Matches are played to the best of three sets.

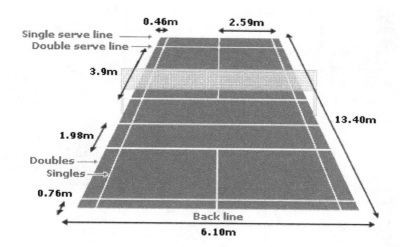

The sport's governing body, the International Badminton Federation (IBF), has introduced a series of rule changes to make the game faster and more entertaining.

Under the old system the first player (or team) to reach 15 points won the set, except in women's singles when the target was 11 points. However both men and women now play up to 21 points. If the score reaches 20-20, the winner is the player or team with a two-point advantage.

And if the score goes up to 29-29, the winner is the first to reach 30 points. In badminton the serve is of huge importance. Points used to be only won on serve.

But this has been scrapped under the new changes, so a player or team can win the point without holding serve. A team now has only one serve in doubles, rather than two under the old rules.

Serving

In singles, players serve diagonally from one service box to another, alternating between the left and right side of the court as points are won. The server always serves from the right-hand box at the start of a game and when they have an even number of points.

They serve from the left-hand court when they have an odd number of points. In doubles, the player on the right always starts the serve and, when a point is won, the players switch sides and the server then serves from the left, continuing to alternate until a serve is lost.

At present a player can only score if they are serving but now points will be awarded to the winner of each rally. Second service in doubles has also been scrapped and best-of-three-set matches will be won by the first to 21 points, instead of 15 for men and 11 for women.

Service action

The shuttlecock must be hit below the server's waist and the racket head must stay below the server's wrist, which means the shot must be played underarm.

The court

Badminton is played indoors, on courts 6.1m wide by 13.4m long. The net posts are 1.55m high.

Courts should have a clearance of 2m on all sides and a ceiling height of 12m.

2017 BADMINTON SINGLES RULES

Rule 1: Facility

All matches will be played on the Main Deck of the Field House. Alcohol and tobacco are not permitted inside the facility.

Rule 2: Player Eligibility

All Intramural Sports eligibility rules apply. Please check the Intramural Sports Rules and Regulations carefully.

Rule 3: Format

1. Badminton uses a "play-by" tournament format, meaning

players will be paired with an opponent for first round matches. Players will have one week to play their matches before advancing to the next round of the tournament. The bracket will be updated the day following the deadline for each round. It is the responsibility of each player advancing in the tournament to set-up the date and time for the next round to be played. Contact information for your next opponent will be provided through IMLeagues.com to facilitate communication for future matches.

2. *All participants are responsible for reporting the results of each match to Ashley Zugschwert upon completion.* Make sure that the winner's name, loser's name, and the scores are all listed in the email. The results must be submitted no later than 11:59 PM on the day of the deadline. All match results will be posted on IMLeagues.com.

Rule 4: Toss

1. Before commencing play, the opponents shall toss a coin and the person the toss shall have the option of:
   o serving first,
   o not serving first, or
   o choosing ends
2. The person losing the toss shall then have the choice of any alternative remaining. Ends are changed after games one and two. If a third game is necessary, ends are changed during the game after one person has scored 11 points.

Rule 5: Scoring System

1. A match consists of best-of-three games to 21 points.
2. At 20 all, the side which gains a two-point lead first wins the game.
3. At 29 all, the side scoring the 30th point wins that game.
4. The side winning a game serves first in the next game.
5. Every time there is a serve, there will be a point scored, *unless that point is replayed.*

6. A two-minute break between each game is allowed.

7. When the leading score reaches 11 points, players may take a 60-second break if needed.

Rule 6: Singles Play

1. At the beginning of the game (0-0) and when the server's score is even, the server serves from the right service court. When the server's score is odd, the server serves from the left service court.

2. If the server wins a rally, the server scores a point and then serves again from the alternate service court.

3. If the receiver wins a rally, the receiver scores a point and becomes the new server. He/she serves from the appropriate service court – left if his/her score is odd, and right if it is even.

Rule 7: Faults

1. If in serving, the shuttlecock is struck above the server's waist.

2. If at the serve, the shuttlecock falls into the wrong receiving court.

3. If the server's and receiver's feet are not within the boundaries of their serving court and receiving court, respectively.

4. If a player touches the net with his/her racquet, person, or clothes.

5. If the shuttlecock is struck in return before it has crossed the net to his/her side. (The follow-through may break the plane of the net.)

Rule 8: General Rules

1. You should not serve until the opponent is ready, but if he/she attempts to return the serve, he/she is considered ready and play continues.

2. If in serving, you miss the shuttlecock, you may serve

again providing your racquet did not make any contact during the attempt.

3. Birdies that hit the net as they cross during play are good and should be played.

4. If, in serving, the shuttle touches the net, it is a "let" provided the service is otherwise good and the birdie is served again.

5. Birdies that fall on the line are considered good.

BADMINTON COURT DIMENSIONS

The length of an entire badminton court is 44 ft. Luckily you only have to cover your side of the net, so 22 ft! The width of the court you must cover is 17 ft in singles, and 20 ft per pair in doubles. The net which equally divides the length of the court should be 5 ft 1in high.

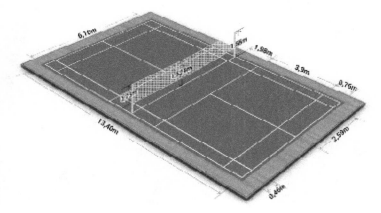

What is 'in' and 'out'?

Whether a particular shot is deemed 'in' or 'out' will differ depending if you are playing singles or doubles. In a singles match the court is often referred to as 'long and thin'. That is, the side tramlines and anything beyond are considered 'out'. This applies for every single shot in a game of singles. The situation in a doubles match is slightly different however.

For a serve in doubles the court is 'short and fat'. Roughly translated, that means that the back tramline is considered 'out', but the side tramline is deemed 'in' - the opposite to the situation in singles.

However this only applies to the serve, as once you are in a rally in a doubles match, anything within the outer court line is considered 'in'. In both singles and doubles, the serve must always cross the front 'service line' however!

4

Badminton Skills & Techniques

BADMINTON SERVE TECHNIQUE

Serving is arguably the most important aspect of the game, as it is the one shot which has to be in every single rally. You have as much time as you need to get ready for it, so there is no excuse for not getting it right. Here we demonstrate and explain three basic types of serve - high server, low serve and flick serve.

Good serves put opponents under pressure, and give servers a better opportunity for success. There are 3 basic serves; High Serve (used in singles only, Low Serve (used in both singles and doubles) and Flick serve (used in doubles).

Badminton serve rules

When it comes to serving there are a few rules that must be obeyed to ensure the serve is legal.

- Players must make contact with the shuttle below the waist
- The racket shaft must be pointing downwards at any degree, ie, the head of the racket must be below the racket hand before making contact with the shuttle.
- Both feet should be on the floor

These rules mean that the shuttle will have to go up in the air to clear the net, because of this, most players now see the serve as a defensive shot. This means it is even more important because if playing a bad defensive shot is likely to lose the point.

Some serves are used more often than others depending if it is a singles or doubles match. The most commonly used serve in singles is the High Serve, if this is played correctly it is difficult for an opponent to hit an effective return. However in doubles the Low Serve is more widely used, maybe because the court is made shorter and wider in doubles the High Serve is not so effective. The flick serve is used unexpectedly to reduce the receivers thinking time.

High serve

This type of serve is most commonly used in singles matches, sometimes known as a long serve. the aim is to send the shuttle high and long and make it drop as close to the furthest back line as possible. This will make it very difficult for an opponent to hit an effective return.

Flick serve

This serve is most widely used in doubles. It is more common to use the backhand serve than the forehand one.The flick serve starts off in the same way as a Low Serve, but a last minute change of pace and flick of the wrist should take the shuttle over the opponents reach, but should not allow them much time to run back and hit an effective return.

The handshake grip should be applied. Adopt an identical position to the Low Serve. The shuttle should be held at waist height and body weight placed on the dominant foot. Take the racket arm into the back swing position and once again cock the wrist.

The next stage is to shift body weight onto the non-dominant foot, and again make use of the wrist and forearm to produce the power and snap the wrist to lift the shuttle above the opponent, catching them out. The shoulders and hips should also rotate to face the opponent within this stage of the serve.

Follow the line of the shuttle with the racket on the follow through, and make sure both arms are up and ready for a possible return.

Low serve

This type of serve is most commonly used in doubles matches. Aim to hit the shuttle so it just clears the net and lands as close to the service line as possible, but it must touch the line at least, if it drops short it will not count. Keeping the shuttle low and short will make it very difficult for an opponent to hit an attacking return.

Return of serve

The return of serve is a very important shot because a good return can force the server into a defensive shot and give the receiver a better chance of winning the point. However be careful not to put absolutely everything into each return, because aiming at the lines and using maximum force, means a player is likely to miss more than they hit. This hands an easy point to the opponent.

To make the return most effective aim the shuttle in the direction of either side tramlines (alley) in the mid-court area. This is because it is more difficult to keep both players on the move, and it also makes the opponents hit an upward (defensive) shot. The aim being to become the attacking team, hitting the shuttle in a downwards direction wherever possible. For returning a flick serve use a followed by a scissors kick.

Backhand low serve

This type of serve has several advantages. It is played from in front of the body so it has a shorter distance to travel, which means it gets to the opponent quicker giving them less thinking time.

Also because the feet are closer together players can stand on tip toes, and still be balanced. This will mean the shuttle can start from a higher position, so it won't have to be hit as high reducing the chance for the opponent to attack.

How: Players should start by holding the racket using the thumb grip.

The stance should be square or slightly staggered with the racket side foot in front of the other foot. The feet and body should be facing the opponent. The shuttle should be held at waist height, and body weight should be distributed between both feet. The back swing for this stroke is much shorter, it can only go back to about level with the body. Make sure the hand and wrist are cocked.

Now shift the weight on to the balls of the feet or on the toes, again with this stroke there is not much use of the wrist and contact should be made around the thigh area.The racket should move in a pendulum action with little follow through.

Drive serve

The drive serve is best used when it is unexpected, because it is hit hard, low and flat so the opposing player has little time to react to it. For the drive serve to be most effective it should be hit to the backhand side of an opponent.

To start the drive serve the racket should be held in the handshake grip. Stand side on facing the forehand side of the court with the non-dominant foot in front of the other. The shuttle should be held in the non-racket hand around waist level.

Most of the body weight should be placed on the dominant (rear) foot.

Take the arm back into the back swing position with the wrist and hand cocked. Body weight should then be shifted on to the non-dominant (front) foot. To produce the pace on this serve a lot of quick wrist action, and forearm rotation is needed. Make contact with the shuttle at thigh level.

On the follow through the racket should carry on through in an upward direction on the same line as the shuttle, and finishing above the non-dominant shoulder. It is then important to get into the ready position with both arms up around chest level.

BADMINTON - VARIANTS

Speed Badminton

This game is inspired from Tennis, Badminton and Squash, and is fast gaining popularity throughout the world. It doesn't require a net or any specific court, and players can play on empty roads, beaches, badminton, or tennis courts.

Two squares, each of 18 feet sides at a distance of 42 feet from each other make the court. The rackets are of length 58-60 cm and similar to Badminton's but the material of strings is different.

The ball, called a speeder, is heavier than a badminton shuttlecock and can shoot through wind better.

Doubles

The doubles match is a variant of Singles Speed Badminton and is played on a single court.

The serving rules are tweaked a bit; so that, all four players get a chance to play the match. A toss or rotating speeder decides who should serve first, and the server rotate among the four players. While the serving player stands at the back court, the other player stands at the front. The rules of faults are similar. The right to serve goes to the one who lost the previous rally.

Black Lighting

With proper lighting and fluorescent equipment, you may play speed badminton even at night. It is a very flexible sport and can be played indoors or outdoors in a court that is painted or pegged off. In some cases a portable court, similar to a carpet court is also used.

When played at night, speed badminton is called Blackminton. Back light, fluorescent paints, glow sticks also called as speed lights, special rackets and speeders fluorescent in color make it possible to play at night.

BACKHAND & FOREHAND CLEAR

The purpose of the forehand clear is used to force your opponent to the rear court. It can be played as an attacking shot or as a defensive shot. The attacking clear is hit faster and flatter into the rear corners.

The defensive clear is hit much higher and despite giving your opponent time to get behind the shuttle - it also gives you more time to get back to a base position.

The overhead clear is played with a throwing action. To execute the shot turn sideways on with the non racket foot forward. Prepare the racket by lining the racket head and the non racket hand up, pointing towards the shuttle. Follow the line of the shuttle back with racket and hand until just before the shuttle is in hitting range. At this stage draw the racket back behind the shoulder and form a throwing position - not dis-similar to that of a javelin thrower.

Reach up and attack the shuttle as early as you can hit it, ideally directly above or slightly in front of the hitting shoulder (somewhere between 12 and 1 o'clock).At this stage the body should turn in, transferring your body weight forward, bringing the racket hip then shoulder through. The follow through should leave the dominant side slightly closer to the net when you have finished the stroke.

During the throwing action the racket should make the sound of a 'whip' or a 'swoosh' as the racket accelerates forward. Advanced players will not only flick the wrist but also pronate the forearm to gain extra racket head speed. (THIS IS OF EVEN MORE BENEFIT WHEN MASTERING A POWERFUL SMASH).

With practice a player can perfect their timing and hit a full length overhead clear with a relaxed grip, enabling them to play the shot over and over without exerting too much energy. Performing the overhead forehand clear is not only important for the shot itself - but it also forms the technical basis for smashes and dropshots. These three strokes between them make up a large percentage of the shots in a game of badminton.

Backhand clear

As with the forehand clear, the purpose of this shot is to get the shuttle over your opponents head and force them as close to the rear court as you can. A backhand clear is usually only played when a player is not in a position to play a forehand ('round the head') shot and as such, this is a defensive shot.

This is one of the toughest shots to play in badminton. As the shuttle is struck behind the body the 'thumb' grip (often confusingly referred to as a backhand grip) should not be used. To enable the correct hitting action the thumb should be diagonally across the grip or placed on the 'bevel' of the grip.

Prior to striking the shuttle the player needs to chassis back towards the rear court and only turn away from the net as the shuttle passes over their head. The player should be looking to lunge with the racket foot in the direction of where the shuttle is due to land. The foot should touch down just before or as the shuttle is struck.

The racket preparation for this shot should be in the form of a loop action whereby the racket head goes over the hand, around and down before accelerating upwards in a 'whip' like action. At the same time extend the shoulder and elbow so that the racket arm is fully extended above the racket shoulder, with the racket pointing up at the sky.

Aim to make contact with the shuttle at the highest point and above the dominant foot - or a near as possible, turning the racket shoulder towards the net in the process. Flick the wrist at the last moment to produce more racket head speed and power.

As a lot of the power comes from the flick of the wrist there is not much follow through on this shot and the racket head should generally finish its swing at the highest point. After hitting the shot switch the feet to once again face the net. Then move back to the mid-court, into the ready position.

BADMINTON SMASH SHOT

The smash is probably the most attacking shot in badminton and if executed well it is probably the most difficult shot to return, just because of the pace and direction put on the shuttle. Here we demonstrate and explain the backhand smash and forehand smash shots.

Backhand smash

The smash is used when an opponent returns the shuttle high but short. The downward angle of the shot is just as important as the speed it is hit at. The advantages of hitting a smash is that it gives the opponent very little time to react and return the shuttle, but if the shuttle is returned this then gives the smasher reduced time to prepare and set themselves for the next shot after hitting a smash. So it is important to choose the correct moment to unleash the smash, as hitting too many can also make players tire quicker. The backhand smash is a top level skill, which only advanced players with a high skill level can execute properly.

BADMINTON LOB TECHNIQUE

The lob shot in Badminton would normally be played from the forecourt in an underarm action.The aim is to lift or 'lob' the shuttle over your opponent and aim to make the shuttle land as near to the baseline as possible without hitting it out.

Forehand lob

As you approach the shuttle move your racket forward with the wrist cocked so that your palm is facing forwards. Move towards the shuttle and take a lunge step with the dominant foot towards where the shuttle is due to land. As the shuttle drops swing the racket forwards underneath the path of the shuttle, striking it upwards whilst straightening the wrist. The follow through should continue up and finish above the non-racket shoulder.

Recover back with the dominant foot first and go back to

the mid-court. The lob can be played very high and deep as a purely defensive shot. It also can be played as a building shot when it is taken earlier (higher up the net) and this shot would be played with only just enough height to go beyond your opponents reach.

Backhand lob

This shot would normally be played from the forecourt in an underarm action. The aim is to lift or 'lob' the shuttle over your opponent and aim to make the shuttle land as near to the baseline as possible without hitting it out.

BADMINTON DROP SHOT

Disguising this shot is the key to its success. To disguise it use a big upper body turn to make the opponent think a clear or smash is going to be hit.The purpose of this shot is to catch your opponent out and make them stretch when playing their reply, hoping to force an unbalanced weak reply.

Although a really effective dropshop can be an outright winner. To execute the drop shot get behind and in line with the shuttle and turn side on to the net. Have the non-racket arm in front of the body and the racket hand should be up behind the head. To enable maximum disguise the racket/body preparation should be near as identical to how you would play a smash or a clear. As the shuttle comes closer extend the racket arm and rotate the shoulders and hips round to face the net. With this shot make contact

with the shuttle out in front of the body but when it is still high in the air. Make sure to direct the shuttle downwards as with a smash but to decelerate the racket head speed - as opposed to accelerating it through. This will ensure the shuttle will drop in the forecourt area.

Backhand drop shot

The drop shot is played from above the head in the same way as the clear except the drop shot is hit with a lot less power.

If played correctly it should have just enough power to clear the net but then drop down to the floor.

This shot is usually only played when the player cannot play a 'round the head' shot with the forehand. Disguising this shot is the key to its success although the strength of a players backhand clear and/or smash will largely dictate the starting position of your opponent i.e. if they are aware that you do not possess a strong backhand clear - as soon as you shape up for a backhand they will most likely move their base position forward in anticipation of a dropshot.

BADMINTON DRIVE SHOT

The drive shot is hit hard on a horizontal or slightly downward path, usually played down the sidelines of the court. This is a safe shot in badminton and if played correctly it will force an opponent to hit an upward return, giving the other player a chance to attack..

Forehand drive

If the shuttle reaches a player between the level of the shoulder and knee, on the forehand side then they could decide to hit a drive shot. If they do decide this is the best option then they need to keep the racket arm up in front of the chest and ensure body weight is spread evenly between both feet.

To get to the shuttle before it drops too low extend the dominant leg towards the shuttle and reach with the racket arm. Then pivot and turn in the direction of the shuttle, have the racket hand palm facing up with the wrist in the cocked position for the back swing. Swing forward and transfer body weight on to the dominant foot. Make sure to extend the racket arm, roll the forearm over in a supination movement and uncock the wrist to provide the power.

The final stage of this stroke is the follow through when the arm should travel in line with the shuttles path, the palm should now be facing down. Then flex and extend the dominant leg to force the body back toward the centre of the court.

Backhand drive

This is a safe shot in badminton and if played correctly it will force an opponent to hit an upward return, giving the other player a chance to attack.

The backhand drive is the same as the forehand version except for the slight grip change, and starting in the back swing with the palm facing down and finishing the stroke with it facing up, opposite to that of the forehand.

To get to the shuttle before it drops too low extend the dominant leg towards the shuttle and reach with the racket arm. Then pivot and turn in the direction of the shuttle, with the wrist in the cocked position for the back swing. This should mean the racket is parallel to the floor. Swing forward and transfer body weight on to the dominant foot. Make sure to extend the racket arm, roll the forearm over in a supination movement and uncock the wrist to provide the power.

The final stage of this stroke is the follow through when the arm should travel in line with the shuttles path. Then flex and extend the dominant leg to force the body back toward the center of the court.

BADMINTON GRIPPING THE RACKET

Badminton grips and how to hold a badminton racket will depend on which shot you are playing and personal preference. The handshake grip and the backhand thumb grip are demonstrated here with the badminton handshake grip being the most common.

Handshake grip

Explanation : This is the most basic grip and used by the majority of players, possibly because it is known as the most comfortable and easiest to use. Another advantage of this grip is that it is very versatile as it can be used for any shot.

How: For the handshake grip players hold the racket out in front of them in the non-playing hand (left hand for a right handed player) and make sure the racket face (strings) is sideways, not facing the sky or floor.

Once in this position players can then place the playing hand (right hand for a right handed player), on the racket face, with the palm against the strings. The next stage is to slide the playing hand down the racket shaft all the way to the bottom of the handle, then wrap the thumb and fingers around the racket making sure the forefinger is slightly apart from the others.

To ensure players are doing it correctly the forefinger and thumb should form a V shape on top of the handle, which in turn should point all the way up the arm to the same shoulder.

Backhand thumb grip

Explanation: This is the most basic grip used in backhand shots which are played in front of the body, possibly because it is known as the most comfortable and easiest to use. Examples of when this grip would be used include the backhand lob ; backhand serves and kill and defence shots. Another advantage of this grip is that it is very versatile as it can be used for any shot. It should however, not be used for behind the body backhand smashes.

How: The backhand grip it is much the same as the handshake grip, but instead of wrapping the thumb round the handle, place it on top of the grip as it is held sideways. This slight change is mainly for added leverage and support, but along with a tighter grip it can also add power, and lessen stress on the hand, wrist, and elbow.

BLOCK SHOT

The block shot is generally used in defense against an opponents smash, but if a player is up at the net it may also be used against a drive shot and can become an attacking shot.

If a player plays a block shot at the net with the racket face closed (pointing at the ground) then this will send the shuttle down quickly making it difficult for the opponent to return.This shot can only be played from the mid court to the net as it uses the power on the opponents shot to take it over the net. If a player tried to play it from the back of the court it would not reach the net unless they swung the racket and then they would be playing a different shot.

Players should already be in the ready position waiting for the opponents return. From this position watch the shuttle off the opponents racket and quickly move in line with the shot. Make sure the racket will intercept the shuttle, and depending on the court position and the height of the return adjust the racket face accordingly. For example if at the net a player may be able to point the face down, however if they are mid court and trying to block a smash they may have to open the face. This will enable the shuttle to clear the net.

The racket should not be swung at all, it is there just to block the shuttle taking all the pace out of the opponents smash or drive. With this shot because the shuttle is traveling so quickly at a player, it will leave little time to assume the correct body position. Players can be blocking the shuttle from peculiar positions but the best way would be to stand square facing the net with the racket out in front of the body.

BADMINTON FOOTWORK

In this chapter will help to improve your grip and give you advice on better footwork. We cover handshake grip, thumb grip, lunge and when they might be used in a game situation.

Ready position

Being in the ready position allows players to move sharply in the direction that the shuttle is traveling. In the ready position a players feet should be square, or slightly staggered depending on the player and how they feel most comfortable.

If a player prefers the staggered position it should be with the dominant foot furthest forward. The feet should be spread about shoulder width apart with the knees slightly bent, and a players weight should be on the balls of the feet.

The racket should be held up in front of the players body, but slightly over to the backhand side.

Some players use the staggered feet position because they feel that it enables them to move from side to side and front to back quicker. The staggered position is very beneficial when a player is returning a serve, as it allows them to anticipate a short serve quicker. However when receiving a serve a players non dominant foot should be furthest forward.

Side Step (Chasse)

This type of step formation can be used to move to any corner of the court, and does allow players to move further and faster, especially towards the net. The next phase is to move the non-dominant foot up behind and slightly closer to the corner, so the back leg is slightly crossed behind the front leg. Then once again move the racket leg forward in the direction of the shuttle, and extend the racket arm out in front of the body.

Moving back: If a player wants to move back towards the backhand side then the first stage is to take the dominant foot back towards the corner they want to move to. The next stage is to bring the non-dominant foot back and behind the dominant, so that the non-dominant foot is closest to the net and the side that they are traveling.

The dominant foot should then take another step back towards the corner and because players can travel further with each step this should take them into the corner, so no extra steps have to be made.

Racket arm and non-playing arm should get higher with each step taken preparing to aim and return the shuttle. Remember to keep both eyes on the shuttle at all times.

Lunge

The lunge is frequently used in badminton. For the purpose of the drill start in the ready position and then stretch the racket foot out. Making sure that the heel touches the floor first place the racket foot on the ground, then move to the toes. Bend the knee of the racket foot taking care to keep the shoulders back and balanced above the hips. Use the none racket arm behind the body to balance the move. During game play the player may need to incorporate a sidestep or a Cross Over Step to move across the court.

Scissor kick

This type of step formation can be used to deliver a powerful shot from the back of the court. In this shot the legs switch position in mid air resembling the closing and then opening of scissors. It is often proceeded by a chasses step, so the player will find they are still moving backwards when the jump is started. Stage one is to jump straight off the ground, then swap your dominant foot with your non dominant foot in mid air with the non dominant foot landing momentarily before the other.

Cross over step

This step is used for travelling quickly across the court. The step-close step footwork uses the non-dominant foot (left foot for a right handed player) as a pivot and the dominant foot as the leading foot. The non-dominant foot is the one that also closes the body away from the shuttle hence the name step-close step.

Players should aim to reach for the shuttle with the dominant arm and leg as this saves time and makes for a faster recovery. Diagonal movement is the fastest way to move from the centre to the corners.

To go from the mid court to the back forehand corner a player must pivot on the non-dominant foot so the toes are pointing towards the side of the court that the player is moving to. Then the dominant leg should take a step towards the forehand back corner.

The next stage is to bring the non-dominant foot across behind the other foot, with the toes and body facing the corner they are traveling to. Both arms should be raised slightly from the ready position to about head height at this stage. Shoulders should be facing forwards.

The last phase of the step-close step is bringing the dominant foot around so the feet are almost square facing the side of the court, with the body also in a side on position. The non-playing arm should be up above the players head out in front of them guiding the shuttle in. The dominant hand should be behind the head with the racket up. Remember to keep both eyes on the shuttle at all times.

Three step return to mid court

This type of step formation can be used to move to any corner of the court, and does allow players to move further and faster, especially towards the net.

From the Net: After hitting a shot from the front of court use the dominant foot to step back with first then the other foot, and then the racket foot again and this should take a player back into the ready position, able to move towards the next shot.

From Back court: After hitting a shot from the back of the court, the legs perform a scissor like action as they leave the floor. This means the dominant leg swings forward and the other leg swings back. The non-dominant leg should then be the one that takes the majority of the weight as a players lands on it first, and this should propel them back towards the middle of the court.

Then use the same 3 step pattern of dominant leg, non-dominant, and dominant leg again to get back into the ready position once again.

BADMINTON NET SHOT

The net shot is played from the net and when played correctly should just tumble over the top of the net and drop as close to the net as possible on the opponents. Try and reach the shuttle before it drops to low to make the shot easier and give the opponent less time to reach the net shot.

Forehand net shot

To reach the shuttle earlier step forward with the dominant foot and reach with the racket arm. Make sure to put the racket face in line with the dropping shuttle. Aim to put slightly more body weight on the front foot.

When in line with the dropping shuttle, cock the wrist, and as soon as the shuttle comes into the hitting area drop the racket head down and quickly lift it to make contact with the shuttle as close to the top of the net as possible. The racket hand palm should be facing up when making contact. The last of the racket lift should come from the shoulder. This should mean the shuttle bounces off the face with no pace on it, making it fall just over the net.

After making contact with the shuttle the racket should keep moving in a upward direction with the shuttle's path. Step back off the front foot to propel the body back to the mid court.

Backhand net shot

This is much the same as the forehand net shot in that to reach the shuttle earlier players need to step forward with the dominant foot and reach with the racket arm. Make sure to put the racket face in line with the dropping shuttle. Aim to put slightly more body weight on the front foot.

When in line with the dropping shuttle, cock the wrist, and as soon as the shuttle comes into the hitting area drop the racket head down and quickly lift it to make contact with the shuttle as close to the top of the net as possible. The last of the racket lift should come from the shoulder. This should mean the racket bounces off the face with no pace on it, making it fall just over the net.

After making contact with the shuttle the racket should keep moving in a upward direction with the shuttle's path. Step back off the front foot to propel the body back to the mid court. The only two differences are using the thumb grip and instead of having the palm facing up when striking the shuttle, it should be facing down at the floor.

BASIC TECHNIQUES

The Grip

How you should hold a badminton racket is like shaking hand with a friend: a normal but firm handshake without trying to crush his fingers.

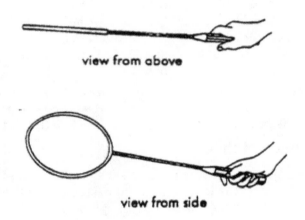

view from above

view from side

Check points: Is the V formed by the thumb and index finger on the top edge of the racket handle?

Are the fingers slightly spread along the handle and not bunched together like a fist? Is the index finger higher up the handle than the thumb?

This is called an *orthodox forehand grip*. This should be a firm but relaxed grip that there must be no feeling of tension in the wrist. You should feel that the control is mainly with the thumb, index finger and little finger. The paramount importance is to get the racket out of the palm of you hand and into your fingers.

This, then, is the forehand grip which is used by most people for shots played on the forehand side of the body and a great many players also find that this is also an all purpose grip which they can used to play shots on the left-hand side of the body as well, ie the backhand. You should be advised to play as much as you can and think about the way you hold your racket while playing. This is not easy in the middle of a game but try to concentrate on the firm but still relaxed grip.

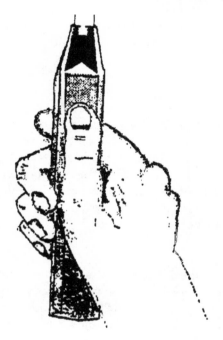

If you are a kind of a player who can cope with all sorts of shots using the same grip, you may not find that it is easier to change the grip slightly to play shorts on the backhand swing.

Check points: You thumb should be resting on the flat side of the handle of the racket and it should be higher up the handle than the index finger.

Press hard with the thumb and you will feel the tremendous amount of leverage you can now exert against the handle and therefore against the backhand face of the racket.

There is a third grip frequently used in badminton which is usually referred to as the 'frying-pan' grip. This grip is achieved by turning the racket from the forehand grip through 90 degrees so that the face of the racket is horizontal to the floor. The V of the thumb and index finger runs down the back, flat edge of the handle. The advantages of this grip are that as the face of the racket is always facing the net, no change in grip is needed to play shots like forehand and the backhand. This grip enable player to execute very sharp dabbing shots at the net.

The Wrist Action

It is the wrist that governs most of the art of deception, an art which must be mastered by all who wish to improve the game. It is the action of the wrist which imparts speed to the head of the racket. The vitally important technique is known as 'cocking' the wrist. This means that for forehand shots, the wrist must be cocked back as far as possible. This can only be done if you have a very relaxed grip. Try this on your shots played overhead on the forehand.

Footwork

To execute a good stroke and swing with good grip, you need to position yourself into the right place in relation to the shuttle. What puts your body into the right position is your feet. Hence, footwork is a subject that should be seriously studied. Good footwork will enable you to get to the shuttle in time to balance; then you can concentrate on playing the accurate shot.

There is no mystique about footwork, for what we really mean by it is court-covering, movement, a means of traveling from one part of the court to another as simply and economically as possible, but quickly.

With anticipation and acute judgment, the advanced player will already have decided, before the shuttle is struck, where he thinks it is going and will have shifted his balance in that direction. Do not allow your feet to become glued to the floor, keep them fidgeting around whilst you wait for your opponent's reply. Hold the racket, with a bent arm, slightly in front of you, and above all, keep the racket head up..

The strokes

The Service

- The short service
- The Flick service
- The high service
- The drive service

Return of Service

The foremost idea in your mind when receiving service should be to hit the shuttle down. The stance you adopted should be the same no matter whether you are playing singles or doubles. You have to be capable of dealing with every type of service. Stand in your receiving court, about 3 feet from the center service line and one to two/three (lady) feet behind the short service. Place your left foot forward so that your feet are comfortable apart and you are evenly balanced. Bend the knees a little and lean slightly forward, so that your weight is mainly over your front foot. Hold your racket in front of you, with the head of the racket up and just above the height of the net, in a forehand grip.

It will take time to develop the ability to stand so close to the short service line and still be able to get back to deal with the flick service.

Your reply to a short serve will depend on how early you can intercept the shuttle. Once you defined it as a short service, push off with the back foot, with the racket raised in front of you, towards the shuttle and do not wait until it reaches you, cut it off ASAP.

If you can meet the shuttle just as it crosses and is still above the net, a sharp dab downwards is the answer. You will not have time for a backswing so you have to rely on a wrist action for power.

When a download stroke is not possible, you will have to drop the racket head beneath the shuttle and stroke it back as close to the tape as possible.

If a high service is delivered, you will have ample time to move back and deal with the shot as you would any other overhead stroke. The best reply is a smash. You may be deceived by a flick service and if you really are deceived you must make the best of it. Move quickly backwards and if you can smash the shuttle. Often you will not be able to get behind a good flick service and you will be left with either a drop shot or a clear. Try to ensure your reply is to a spot that your opponent have left unguarded.

To return a drive service, because a drive service is so flat and fast, the best return is to put the face of your racket in its path to allow the shuttle to bounce off it. Use your wrist to flick it downwards or upwards to a suitable space or aim directly to your opponent so he will not have sufficient time to return.

The Overhead Forehand Strokes

- Smash
- Clear
- Drop Shot: Slow/Fast

The Overhead Backhand Strokes

Although most of the advanced user can deal with smash, clear and drop shot with forehand as well as backhand, the clear is the most important in the group when backhand is played. Most player especially novices find the backhand corner of the court rather difficult to cope with and naturally their opponents tend to take advantage of this fact.

A sound backhand clear has therefore come to be recognized as the main defensive measure to be taken. The ability to execute an effective backhand clear depends entirely on a very powerful wrist flicking action and perfect timing.

Very few player can be really effective with the fackhand smash unless it is a sitter near the net. It is not a shot to be played from the base line area nor even from as far back in court as you would expect to be able to play your forehand smash. Play it from mid or forcourt area and place the shuttle in proper position to make it an effective skill.

The Drives

Underarm Strokes

Your aim in returning a smash is to play the shuttle into your opponent's court, in such a way that he will have difficulty in making a good reply. Prepare for smash by adopting an open stance, biased towards the backhand with your right foot just in the lead. Bend your knees slightly and keep on the balls of your feet. You cannot afford to be glued to the floor for you will have to move rapidly if your opponent does not smash. With a backhand grip, bring the racket across your body, with its head opposite your left shoulder. Keep the racket head up because you have to be able to move into the smash and take it early. With experience and as your timing improves, move forward and try to take the shuttle earlier and higher. There will not be much time for an appreciable backswing but with the racket held up you are half way there.

For the lob to the back of the court, the action will be just as in your underarm clear, more wrist movement will be needed.

For the drop, just over the net would be more effective. With practice your timing and touch will improve so that you will be able to pop the shuttle just over the net.

For the drive, the power combined with the speed of the shuttle make the drive return to a smash a very formidable shot. You will have to get your eye in and play the shuttle early for the shot to be fully effective.

Round The Head

Tactics

Rule: play to his weakness; make him play to your strength.

- Angle of Return

- Narrow/Wide
- Single Play
- Double Play
- Men's Doubles

In men's double, the accent is on attack and pace. The frequency with which you can keep the shuttle going down and the understanding you have with your partner will determine your success. In singles and mixed you largely had to play for your openings by careful placements and a variation of pace before you could finish off a rally because there is so much ground to cover on your own and in mixed you have a partner at the net in a very vulnerable position in front of you. These considerations do not apply in men's double. Assuming you have a partner of equal strength and ability and between you the whole court filled. You can afford to force openings with sheer pace alone.

You must try to attack the whole time, never forget this.

You should play front and back as this is the only attacking system. Some men do adopt a side by side formation. The drawbacks are obvious. Each partner must play a mostly defensive game because even when he smashes he has to rush in to take any weak return at the net, probably arriving rather late. It is also allowing your opponent to single out one palyer and work him into the ground whilst never allowing his partner to hit the shuttle at all.

The idea of switching positions, depending on whether you are attacking or defending is not difficult to follow but it often breaks down because the players are slow in adjusting their formation.

- Mixed Doubles
- Women's Doubles.

BADMINTON SINGLES TACTICS

This guide will teach you how to choose the right shots in singles, and how to position yourself to cover the court well.

Most tactics guides contain little tactical content, and read like an inventory of shots: use all the different shots to pressure your opponent. Well, yes. But *why* choose one shot rather than another? What is the tactical difference between a clear and a drop shot?

How would *you* answer that question? Would you say something anodyne, such as: clears move your opponent into the rearcourt, and drops move him into the forecourt; or they are both good shots, and it's best to vary your shots?

If so, then you don't yet understand the nature of these shots. You can learn about them more deeply later in this guide (clears and drops).

This guide contains a large amount of detailed information, so you may prefer to digest it over more than one sitting.

The basics

The first few pages explain the fundamental ideas:

- The basic strategy in singles: movement pressure
- The idea of a central base position and how it should be adjusted
- The principle of hitting to the corners, and the differences between corners
- Hitting to the middle as a defensive resource

Apart from just describing these concepts, I provide deep analysis of why they work. For example, my page on hitting to the same corner includes extensive analysis of this tactic's psychological effect. Even if you are familiar with these basic tactics, you may still learn something useful.

Building and winning shots

The next two sections, building shots and winning shots, give detailed advice about individual shots. These sections answer the question, Why choose one shot rather than another?

In both these sections, I explain the merits of each shot, and the tactical consequences of choosing different angles or trajectories. I also explain how certain shots are connected, and offer tactical analysis of sequences of shots.

Tactics depend on skills

This guide will assume that you have a complete set of stroke skills and are physically fit enough for the game.

You will need to adapt your tactics to cover up weaknesses. For example: if your high serve is inconsistent and rarely reaches the back tramlines, then you should probably never use it. Try a low serve instead.

You can of course improve your performance by training to eliminate those weaknesses. But it's too late for this when you're playing a match! In competition you must adapt your tactics for your *current* capabilities.

THE BASIC STRATEGY: MOVEMENT PRESSURE

In singles, the basic strategy is to apply maximum *movement pressure* to your opponent. This means that you force him to cover distance rapidly and change direction.

By forcing your opponent to move quickly about the court, you create situations where he will reach the shuttlecock late and have difficulty playing an effective shot. Once he plays a weak shot, you have the choice between pushing him even farther out of position, or attempting to win the rally immediately.

Here is a simple example of creating movement pressure:

1. You play a clear. Your opponent is forced to move into the rearcourt.

2. Your opponent plays a drop shot.

3. You play a net shot. Your opponent is forced to move into the forecourt.

By this simple sequence of shots, you forced your opponent to move into the rearcourt, and then back to the forecourt. This puts some pressure on his movement ability.

Doubles strategy doesn't work in singles

Many players believe that they can win singles just by applying their doubles smash. This is a fundamental mistake. In singles you have no partner to cover the net, so doubles-style attack is much less effective.

Doubles attack involves creating *shot-making pressure*: when defending a smash, you don't have much time to position your racket and it's easy to lose control of the shot. You're also placed under tremendous pressure by the front player, who will try to punish any net replies.

The attackers in doubles must move about the court rapidly. In particular, the back player jumps all over the place, to ensure he can keep on smashing.

So doubles attackers accept *movement pressure* in return for the *shot-making pressure* that they apply to their opponents. Because the attackers can work together to cover their court, this exchange usually turns to the attackers' advantage: in doubles, shot-making pressure usually beats movement pressure.

In singles it's the other way around: movement pressure usually beats shot-making pressure.

It's much more difficult to cover the court in singles, because there's only one of you!

This makes movement pressure much more effective in singles than in doubles. Shot-making pressure is also less effective because you no longer have a partner covering the net. After you smash, your opponent can turn the tables simply by blocking the shuttlecock back to the net.

BADMINTON BASICS FOR BEGINNERS

Badminton Gripping Technique

This page teaches you the basic badminton gripping technique. Before you even enter the badminton court, are you holding your racquet correctly?

How to Hold a Badminton Racket

The correct way of holding a racquet is as simple as a FRIENDLY HANDSHAKE. Imagine the grip of the racquet as a hand approaching to shake your hand. Go ahead and hold the racquet as if you're shaking someone's hand.

Your thumb should be pressing comfortably against one of the wider surface of the racquet grip while the rest of your hand holds the racquet as if you're shaking a person's hand.

The way you hold your racket can affect the flexibility of your wrist.

In order to execute strong badminton strokes with high accuracy, your wrist needs to be flexible.

To achieve this, make sure you:

- Do not grip your racquet too tightly. This will make your wrist less flexible in rotating and flicking.

- Use ONLY your thumb, index, and middle finger to control the racket. Your last 2 fingers should rest comfortably on the badminton grip to balance the weight of the racquet. By doing this, it enables your wrist to be more flexible and move more freely.

Alright that's just about the basics of holding the racquet.

Forehand Grip and Backhand Grip

Next thing you need to learn is the forehand and backhand grip.

Basically you'll need to use the:

- Forehand grip to hit forehand shots.
- Backhand grip to hit backhand shots.

The forehand and backhand grip looks almost the same. There's only one slight difference – the placement of your fingers. You'll understand this when I explain more about these 2 badminton gripping technique below.

Forehand Badminton Gripping Technique

Your thumb does not necessarily have to press against the wider surface of the badminton grip for a forehand stroke. Your index finger should be the one "in control" in a forehand stroke. This simply means using your index finger to push the racquet forward while doing a forehand stroke.

However, rest your thumb comfortably anywhere near the wider surface of the badminton grip to enable you to change to a backhand grip quickly.

Backhand Badminton Gripping Technique

The key to perform strong backhands depends on how you hold your racquet. The true power of a badminton backhand shot comes from the push of your thumb.

A backhand stroke requires you to USE YOUR THUMB. So you should now press your thumb on the wider surface of the badminton grip. Relax your index finger and move it closer to your middle finger.

The backhand grip will look like you're doing a 'thumbs up'.

Generating power with Finger Action...

Just remember, finger action plays an important role in generating strength for a badminton stroke.

- Push your index finger forward for forehand strokes.
- Push your thumb forward for backhand strokes.

Pro Players Switch Grips Quickly

You should learn to switch quickly from the forehand to backhand grip, and vice versa.This enables you to quickly prepare for your strokes and hit the shuttle at the highest point, hence delivering quality shots.

Effective Badminton Footwork: A Complete Guide for Beginners

Many people neglect badminton footwork because it might not seem important at all.

You might hear some people say "why care about footwork when I can do a 300km/h smash". Are you thinking that way too? However I would say that the footwork is THE most important skill you should master. It's even more important than smashing!

This is because an effective and organised footwork provides superb speed and agility which enables the player to move around the badminton court swiftly and return every shuttlecock. So what if you can do a 300km/h smash when you cannot even reach the shuttlecock in time?

Playing badminton is all about speed. The shuttlecock can move extremely fast and you must move faster than the shuttlecock to be able to hit it.

Effective Movement On the Court

Always remember your base (starting point) will be at the red dot in the middle. The arrows indicates the possible movements around the court.

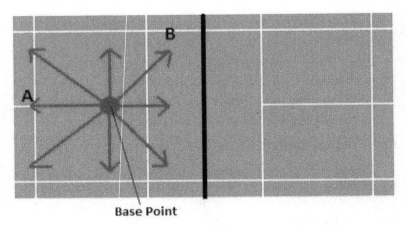

Base Point

Every time you move away from your base to hit the shuttle, you MUST QUICKLY return to your base to prepare yourself for your opponent's shot

For instance, you move to point A to take a shuttle and then stay there. Your opponent then returns the shuttle back to you at point B. You are less likely able to get to point B in time from point A.

Conversely, if you quickly return to your base after hitting the shuttle at point A, you will definitely be able to return the shuttle at point B.

Tips on How to Move Effectively

There are many ways of moving out there but does this mean you have to know and follow all? No, just be comfortable with your own style of moving around the court.

However, there are a few tips that I would like to share on your badminton footwork

- Take ONLY 2-3 steps when moving to the *back* of the court.
- Stretch ONLY 1 step towards the *sides* of the court.
- Take ONLY 2-3 steps to the *front* of the court.
- Are you a beginner? Does it seem difficult to take so few steps? No worries, the key is to stretch your legs as wide

as possible while maintaining a good balance. If you are a beginner, take more steps. Then slowly reduce the amount of steps you take as you move faster while maintaining good balance.

- Maintain your balance: While one of your hands will be holding the racquet, keep the other hand wide open. Not because it looks cool, it is because it helps in balancing. This enables you to return to your base quickly.

- Good stance:. When you're in a ready position (before your opponent serves), make sure one leg is in front and one leg behind, opened slightly wide *(refer to the picture above)*.

- If the shuttle is served to the front, use your toes of your back leg to push your bodyweight to the front.

- If the shuttle is served to the back, use your front leg toes to push your bodyweight to the back. This enables you to move fast once the shuttle is served.

Important Advice

The idea is to quickly move to take the shuttle and then quickly return to your base.

Agility is important, but body balance is *equally* important. If you do not have good body balance, you'll lose time trying to stabilise yourself — in turn this gives you less time to return to your base.

All the above is merely a guide. There are no BEST ways for badminton footwork, you should move in a way you are comfortable with and keep practising.

Badminton Strokes

It's VERY IMPORTANT to perform your badminton strokes correctly in order to execute quality badminton shots.

Remember, you MUST master these basic strokes in order to play like a pro!

Basically a stroke is the swing motion of your racket arm. It is not a badminton shot. However you'll need to perform these strokes to hit certain shots. The power of any badminton shot comes from how well you perform your strokes (*swing motion*). A beginner should FIRST learn how to perform the CORRECT strokes.

Why is it important to perform the correct strokes from the start?

It is impossible to hit strong backhand shots in badminton if you perform the wrong backhand stroke.

Let's look at an example... John did not learn the correct badminton backhand stroke and have been hitting backhands using 'his own style' for several years.

After few years of wrong backhand stroke technique, John finds it difficult to 're-learn' the correct backhand stroke technique. He is already too used to the wrong technique. He has developed a bad habit!

Why are bad habits BAD in badminton?

1. It restricts you from performing quality badminton shots.
2. Bad habits often become your weakness. You perform your overhead backhand strokes wrongly. There is no way you could hit a backhand clear to the baseline. The only shot you can do is a straight backhand drop. Your opponent knows about it. After hitting the shuttle to your backhand area, your opponent rush to the forecourt and waits for your drop shot.

Once you have developed the habit of performing your strokes, it's very difficult to change the way you perform these strokes in the future. Therefore, it's important that you learn the correct strokes right from the start (*all types of strokes, not only the backhand.*

If you think you have 'bad habits', it is never too late. You'll find some useful guides on badminton strokes below to help you become a better a player. Of course, practice is always the key to perfection.

The basic strokes are:

- Overhead Forehand Stroke
- Overhead Backhand Stroke
- Underarm Forehand Stroke
- Underarm Backhand Stroke.

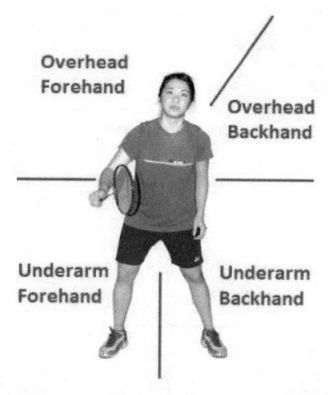

When the shuttle flies towards a particular area around your body, you'll need to use different strokes to hit the shuttle. The picture above shows you the 4 different areas around your body where you're required to use the 4 different badminton strokes to return the shuttle.

Badminton Serve

A badminton serve can be performed using 2 methods (high serve and low serve), depending on where you want the shuttlecock to land. There are certain rules that you must follow when making a service. Checkout the badminton service fouls to avoid it.

The Importance of a Good Badminton Serve

A WEAK serve often creates a chance for your opponent to execute an attacking shot. Therefore it's important to know how to serve properly so that you will not lose a point after making a service.

The High Badminton Serve

This type of serve is usually executed when you want the shuttle to land at the back end of the court. A *good* high serve must have the shuttle dropping steeply downwards at the back end of the court.

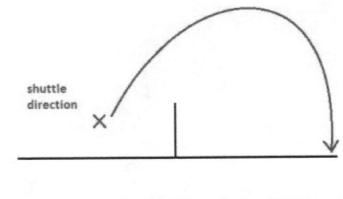

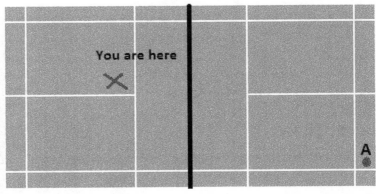

A high serve will prevent your opponent from executing a strong smash. Instead, a lob or a drop is more expected from your opponent (unless they can do a jump smash).

Try to serve the shuttlecock to your opponent's backhand area. The objective is to force your opponent to use his backhand. This is because most badminton players, even world class player, have weaker backhands (compared to their forehands)

For example, you're standing at X. You are about to make a high serve... and your opponent is right handed. In that case, direct the shuttle to drop at point A.

This will *force your opponent to use the backhand* and hence there's a higher chance that he'll return a weak shot.

If your hit it to your opponent's backhand area, but he/she refuses to use the backhand, he will then have to move further away from his base! This gives you the chance to exploit an opportunity to control the game if your opponent does not have good badminton footwork.

Let me show you how to do a *high serve...*

- Hold the head of the shuttlecock with its head facing downwards so that the shuttlecock will drop straight down.

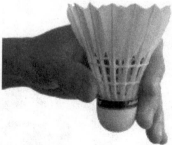

- Stand sideways (the side of your body facing the net) and relax your racquet arm (arm that is holding the racquet).
- Let go of the shuttlecock and swing your racquet arm upwards. As you do this, twist your waist to the extent that your body faces the net. Flick your wrist towards the direction you want the shuttle to land (Flick your wrist *upwards,* so that the shuttlecock will fly high).

- Your back leg should lift up naturally (with your toes touching the ground).

The high serve is useful against opponents who cannot perform strong smashes from the back of the court. However, some badminton players (especially taller players) can execute powerful smashes even from the back of the court (usually with a jumping smash). If this is the case, consider using the *low serve* instead. This is also the reason why professional players nowadays prefer using the low serve.

The Low Badminton Serve

The low serve is used when you want the shuttlecock to land in front of the court (in front of your opponent).

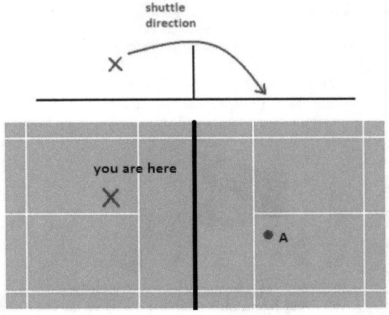

A GOOD low serve will have the shuttlecock flying JUST ABOVE THE NET.

If not, your opponent will have the chance to dash forward and smash the shuttle down to you. A low serve, when executed beautifully, prevents your opponent from making an offensive shot. Unlike the high serve, you can let the shuttle drop anywhere in front (forehand area or backhand area of your opponent) Neither makes a difference because it does not disrupt your opponent's footwork. As a start, practice serving so that the shuttle drops right in front of your opponent (point A in picture above).

Let me show you how to do a *low serve...*

- Hold the feather of the shuttlecock with the head of the shuttlecock facing downwards.

- Position the racquet behind the shuttlecock.

- Step slightly forward with your right (left) leg if you are right handed (left handed).

- As you let go of the shuttlecock, flick your racquet lightly while pushing your thumb forward towards the direction you want the shuttle to land. The power comes mainly from the push of your thumb and the slight flick of your wrist.

The Flick Serve ("Fake" Low Serve)

The "fake" low badminton serve can also be used to trick your opponent (deceive your opponent to expect a low serve).

When you stand in a low serve position, your opponent would probably expect a low serve. However, push your thumb and flick your wrist harder so the shuttlecock flies HIGH and heads to the back of the court!

Well, knowing how to serve is one thing. *Practising* is another. If you want to make perfect serves, keep practising until you don't make any mistakes!

Badminton Stance

What's a badminton stance?

It is the way you stand when retrieving certain shots from your opponent. This may be your first time hearing of this term. So far I have not seen any online badminton resource that covers this topic. Let me know in the comments section below if you use a different term for this. But I thought it's good information to share with you especially if you want to improve your games.

Basically there're 3 types of badminton stances, They are:

- Attacking Stance
- Defensive Stance
- Net Stance

Using the correct stance to retrieve your opponent's shots will definitely give you an advantage in a rally.

Attacking Stance

You'll need to use this stance whenever you hit an overhead forehand stroke.

To get into the attacking stance,

- Turn your body facing the side of the court.
- Place your racket leg behind; your non-racket leg forward.
- Both legs should be shoulder width apart.
- Raise your racket and non-racket arm

Hitting forehand strokes via the attacking stance enables you to hit powerful shots. It also enables you to recover quickly after you perform your shot.

When to use?

Whenever your opponent lifts or clear the shuttle high up to you, move towards the shuttle and adopt the attacking stance.

Defensive stance

The key to strong defense is to retrieve your opponent's smash via the defensive stance.

To get into the defensive stance,

- Face your body to the front of the court.

- Place your racket in front of you, around waist height, and pointing slightly forward. .
- Raise your non-racket arm for better balance.

When you're on a defensive stance, you can cover wider angles. For example, you'll find it a lot easier to retrieve smashes hit to your body, left hand side, or right hand side.

When to use?

Whenever you hit a High Clear or perform a High Serve, move to your base position and adopt the defensive stance. Ideally, you want to be at your base position before your opponent hits the attacking shot.

Just in case you want more, here's a page on badminton defense.

Net Stance

The net stance enables you to take the shuttle at the highest point when you're at the net. When exchanging net shots, every millisecond counts! So make sure you take the shuttle as early as possible.

To get into the net stance,

- Place your racket foot forward; non-racket foot at the back.
- Place your racket in front of your body, slightly above waist height.
- Raise your non-racket arm for body balance.
- Place your body weight slightly forward and get ready to pounce forward.

When to use?

Normally the only time you need to adopt the net stance is after you perform a Tumbling Net Shot. Your body's posture will naturally be on the badminton net stance after you hit the tumbling net shot. So STAY THERE and be ready to pounce forward to perform the net kill if your opponent hits a net shot.

Types of Badminton Clear

The badminton clear (known as lobbing in most Asian countries) is the most important badminton shot, especially in a singles game. In a singles game, players use the clear more than any other types of shots. A high defensive clear prevents your opponent from smashing from a good angle. If your clear sends the shuttle right to your opponent's baseline, it's considered a "good" defensive clear. On this page, I'll walk you through the different types of clears and provide tutorials for each of them. But first, let me illustrate the difference between a good clear and a poor quality clear.

Good vs Poor Badminton Clear

Good Defensive Clear

The shuttlecock drops steeply to the baseline. Your opponent is forced to take the shuttle at point X, which is near the baseline. He won't have a good angle for a smash from so far back of the court.

Poor Defensive Clear

The shuttlecock travels flatter towards the baseline. Your opponent can intercept at point X, which is nearer to the mid court. A smash taken at point X can be dangerous and difficult to defend.

Objective of the Defensive Clear

The objective of the Defensive Clear is to 'create' time for yourself. When you're not able to keep up with the pace of the rally, hitting High Clears deep into your opponent's baseline would be a smart choice.

This is an easy badminton technique. Beginners should master the Defensive Clear using all 4 badminton strokes to play longer rallies against your opponents.

How to Hit the Defensive High Clear

The high Defensive Clear is usually performed with the FOUR common badminton strokes. The following leads to my tutorial pages on the Clear.

How to Play the Forehand Badminton Smash

Flight Trajectory of the Smash

- It is an offensive shot executed from the rear court.

- It travels downwards to your opponent's side.

Get into position and adopt the Forehand Grip.

If you intend to hit the smash, you should move quickly towards the shuttle. In professional badminton, we call this 'injection of pace'.

Ideally, your body should face the side of the court. Both your feet should also point sideways.

Forehand Grip

Stand on a firm position.

If you're not on good balance, your smash won't be strong because your body will concentrate on balancing first rather than doing a strong swing.

Raise your Racket Arm and Non-Racket Arm.

Make sure you stretch your racket arm as far back as possible. This will help ensure you perform a full arm swing.

At the same time, raise your Non-Racket Arm to balance out the weight of your Racket Arm. This is VERY IMPORTANT to help you maintain body balance.

You are now ready to hit the smash. This is how you should look like...

Take the shuttle at the highest point possible.

This creates a steep angle for your smash.

Hit the Shuttle with a Full Arm Swing.

Take a deep breath. Stretch out your chest to the widest extend possible. Stretch out your Non-Racket Arm.

Then swing your racket forward as you exhale. At the same time, contract your abs. Shuffle your Racket Foot to the front.

Follow Through with your Swing.

After you hit the shuttle, follow through and complete your

swing. Your body should face forward after you swing your racket. Maintain body balance and recover.

Common Misconceptions

Every one can smash. It's simple...

Swing your racket forward as hard as you can and there you go... A Smash!

Knowing how to smash doesn't make you a pro. Smashing with the right technique is the key to bring your badminton skills to the next level.

Smashing hard doesn't win you points. But smashing smart does!

On this page, you'll learn how to execute the smash smartly and correctly.

Important Tips and Advice

- Perfect your Overhead Forehand Stroke: In order to produce quality smashes, you'll need to get your Overhead Forehand Stroke right.
- Perfect Your Technique for Smashing: Good technique is super important when doing the badminton smash.

When you begin to train your smash, try to do soft badminton smashes first to familiarize yourself with the correct technique.

Once you are familiar with the technique, gradually increase the power of your smash over time.

It's VERY important that you do not start off using your full strength. Your focus will be diverted to doing strong swings and balancing rather than executing the correct technique.

- Loosen up your body. You won't get the technique right if your body is too tensed. Relax your muscles. Do not grip your racket too tightly.
- Non-racket Arm: I find this a common mistake among most people. Don't forget to use your Non-Racket Arm for body balance. You should make it a habit! Besides balance, it'll make your smash look cool!

• Do not smash every time! Another common mistake. Maybe because most people think that the badminton smash is the 'coolest' shot.Always remember the objectives of a smash…Apart from that, smash ONLY when you arrive quickly at the shuttle.

There's no point smashing if you can't get into position in time.A badminton smash is like a double edged sword, it's difficult for your opponent to defend it. BUT if your opponent manages to defend it, you may need to regain your balance quickly to be able to retrieve the returned shot.

Badminton Net Play

Badminton net play is a vital skill when you're playing along the net with your opponent. This is a fairly difficult skill to master because you need EXTREMELY good control over your racket.

If you're good at net play, you can easily win a rally at the front of the court, by performing the tumbling net shot or the badminton net kill.

Don't worry so much if you don't get what I'm saying right now. I will guide you through with simple steps and you'll master the various badminton net play skills with enough practice.

Steps to Master Badminton Net Play

To master this badminton skill, you'll need:

1. Good badminton footwork to bring you quickly to the front of the court to return the shuttle. Always try to take the shuttle when it's still high in the air. In this case, hit the shuttle at the highest point possible near the net.

If the shuttle is near the badminton net and is still high up, JUST TAKE YOUR CHANCE TO SMASH!

Engage in badminton net play only when your opponent returns a perfect drop shot, or if he gives you a net shot and you wish to return another net shot.

2. Good control of your racket. First, make sure that you're holding your racket the correct way. Review your badminton basics to maximise your badminton net play skills.

Good control over your badminton racket is important to ensure you exert just enough power into your net shot (and not too much power, but sufficient power for the shuttle fly across just above the net).

You'll have to practice a few times and figure out how much strength to exert for a net shot; and also find out where's the best point to 'slice' your racket against the shuttle.

Other Useful Tips for Effective Badminton Net Play:

- Take the shuttle at the highest point possible.
- Exert appropriate strength to send the shuttle across the other side (preferably having the shuttle fly RIGHT ABOVE THE NET)

Types of Net Shots

The following are the tutorials for the various badminton net play skills.

The Tumbling/Spinning Net Shot

Badminton Spinning Net Shot (a.k.a. Tumbling Net Shot): Force your opponent to lift the shuttle high up to you. If you can play extremely good spinning net shots, the net shot itself can be a 'killer shot' and you'll find yourself winning rallies at the front of the net.

The Net Kill

Badminton Net Kill (Offensive): When your opponent returns a weak net shot, strike it swiftly with net kill!

The Net Lift

Badminton Net Lift (Defensive): The net lift is an important defensive shot. Send the shuttle to the back of the court with a net lift! This skill is important to keep you out of trouble if your opponent plays very well along the net.

Get the Basics Right

I personally consider this as the biggest challenge in badminton, even more challenging than doing a jump smash!

I suggest you learn this skill AFTER you're familiar with all your basic badminton strokes.

Put your racket near the net and let the shuttle 'BOUNCE' over the other side of the court whenever you get a front shuttle.

Get a feel of where's the best point to touch the shuttle in order for it to 'bounce' just above the net.

When you already master the technique of 'bouncing' the shuttle to the other side of the court, you might want to bring your net play skills to the next level.

How to Win Rallies with Badminton Net Play

The basic idea is to:

- Force your opponent to the front of the court. This is usually done by hitting a drop shot (if you're at the back of the court) or hit a spinning net shot (if you're at the front of the court)
- Play along the net with your opponent until he decides to lift the shuttle high up

If your opponent:

- Returns a weak net shot (shuttle flies high above the net), perform the net kill
- Returns an extremely good net shot (shuttle hits the top of the badminton net and tumbles over to your side of the court), perform the net lift

Badminton net play is mainly used to FORCE your opponent to lift the shuttle high in the air, so that you can execute a strong attacking shot.

The competition is based on who gives up playing along the net and lifts the shuttle. If you give up playing along the net and lift the shuttle, you are inviting your opponent to attack you. However, you're sometimes forced to lift the shuttle if your opponent plays very well along the net. If you're good at playing near the net, your opponent may decide not to engage in badminton net play. This forces your opponent to "lift" the shuttle high up, giving YOU a chance to produce an offensive shot!

TECHNOLOGY

Badminton is fastest racket game and now days there are great changes in the playing pattern and speed. Technological innovations have a great influence in today's game of badminton. In this paper the influence of technology is explained, that how the technology has changed the standard of the game by use of technology and new material in construction of the equipments like court, racket, shuttle, shoes and clothing. The game or badminton is now more skill and technology oriented. Better quality courts are used now for better grip of shoes and power cushion is used in shoes according to presser points, light weight and titanium made very powerful rackets are used now, much better aerodynamic shuttles are used in a lot of variety according to the conditions. Video technology is the most important these days for complete analysis of the skill performed by the player, video recording and analysis is very useful for improvement of the technique of skill accusation. So technology has developed lot in the game of badminton.

5

Equipment

GETTING STARTED - BASIC BADMINT ON EQUIPMENT AND GEAR

Although it wouldn't hurt to have chic shoes and smart looking attire, you should be looking for function over aesthetics when it comes to your badminton equipment. We cover the four basic equipment and gear required for a game of badminton.

Badminton Racket

Badminton rackets can be made from several types of materials. Depending on the material selection, this can result in different combinations of racket weight, balance points and string tensions. With so many different combinations, it will take time to decide which is most suited for your playing style.

Instead of making purchases online, pop by a badminton shop. Ask for assistance and select a racket that you feel comfortable with. Swing the racket around to get a good feel of its overall weight and grip. Some popular badminton brands are Yonex, ProKennex, Wilson, ProTech and Li-Ning.

Shuttlecock

There are two types of shuttlecocks - plastic and feathered shuttlecocks. Plastic shuttlecocks are far more durable compared to the feathered types which are commonly used. However, plastic shuttlecocks are only recommended for beginners who are just starting out.

This is because feathered shuttlecocks are expensive and fray easily especially if the wrong technique is used. Hence, plastic shuttlecocks are good for beginners to use for training. Plastic shuttlecocks are usually used by young children who play badminton for recreation.

Plastic shuttlecocks tend to travel shorter distances as they are heavier.

Hence, they are good for building strength as you make the transition to feathered shuttlecocks. Most people will progress to using feathered shuttlecocks as they are used at all competitive tournaments.

Badminton Shoes

Badminton shoes are designed to give you better traction and grip to stop in time to return a shot. They should also be lightweight have good cushioning to absorb impact when you jump or land.

Regular players will find heel cups useful to prolonging the lifespan of your shoes. Do not wear jogging shoes as they usually lack grip and traction. You might end up crashing through the badminton net if you are unable to stop in time to receive a drop shot.

Badminton Attire

For casual to non-competitive players, a comfortable pair of shorts and cotton or dri-fit t-shirt is sufficient. Some players may want to equip themselves with hand grips, wrist bands and ankle guards. Each of these items serve a purpose and might also add a dash of colour to the entire get-up.

When it comes to badminton equipment, select what is appropriate before turning your attention to aesthetics. With this in mind, have fun shopping and gearing up for your next match.

LIST OF BADMINTON EQUIPMENT

In badminton, players use rackets to hit a shuttlecock back and forth over a net. Badminton equipment must meet certain rules and specifications. The Badminton World Federation’s Laws of Badminton provide a standard for equipment in competitive badminton.

Shuttles

Players should have several shuttles, also known as “birdies” or “shuttlecocks,” to use in a match. You can use natural, feathered shuttles or synthetic, non-feathered shuttles in badminton.

According to the Badminton World Federation’s Laws of Badminton, feathered shuttles should have 16 feathers fixed to a cork base. The feathers should measure between 2 ½ and 2 ¾ inches long.

The feathers’ tips should form a circle with a diameter measuring between 2 ¼ and 2 2/3 inches. Synthetic shuttles should simulate feathers with synthetic materials. Both feathered and synthetic shuttles should have a base that measures about 1 inch in diameter. The shuttle should weigh about .16 to .19 oz. Players should test the shuttles for speed and flight before each match.

Racket

Badminton rackets consist of stringed hitting surface attached to a thin shaft and a handle. The racket must have a flat face, with a uniform pattern of overlapping strings. According to the Badminton World Federation’s Laws of Badminton, the racket’s stringed area should not exceed 11 inches in length or 8 2/3 inches in width. The racket’s overall length, including the handle, shaft, and face, may not exceed 26 ¾ inches in length. The racket must not exceed 9 inches in width at its widest point. Early badminton racket manufacturers produced only wooden rackets, but modern manufacturers produce rackets with frames made out of aluminum alloy, titanium, steel, and composite materials.

Net

The net plays an important role in badminton matches. The Badminton World Federation’s Laws of Badminton provide specific standards for net height, width, and construction. An official badminton net must measure 5 feet high in the center, and 5 feet, 1 inch at the sides. The net attaches to vertical posts on either side of the court. The net should measure 30 inches from bottom to top, and must consist of a uniform, dark-colored mesh. The net should have a white tape running along the top to make the net’s full height visible to players and officials.

BADMINTON RACKET

Modern Badminton Rackets are light in weight and don't weigh more than 100 grams. The frame of the Racket can be made of common metals like steel or aluminium. Sometimes rackets are made of alloys, tough carbon fiber, ceramic, or boron. Its length does not exceed 680mm and width does not exceed 230 mm.

Shuttlecock

Sixteen feathers fixed in a cork base enveloped in a thin leather sheet make a shuttlecock. Interestingly, the best Badminton Shuttlecocks are made from feathers from the wing of a goose. The shuttle weighs between 4.74 to 5.50 grams.

Badminton Shoes

A good pair of Badminton Shoes provide good grip, cushioning and some flexibility at the forefoot.

Badminton Accessories

The commonly used Badminton Accessories are Grip, Badminton Clothes, Socks, Wrist Band and Head Band.

Grip

A grip made of cloth or synthetic fiber absorbs sweat and provides you a drier feel.

Badminton Clothes

Comfortable T-shirts and shorts, that don't hinder your movement are ideal to play Badminton. A cotton round-neck or a collar t-shirts with a pair of light shorts are usually preferred.

Socks

Wear a pair of thick cotton socks as they help to absorb sweat. They also prevent your feet from slipping inside your shoes. Avoid wearing Nylon socks that don't absorb sweat.

Wrist Band

If you perspire a lot, you may consider getting a wrist band that prevents your sweat from flowing to your racket handle.

Head Band

Wear a Head Band if you wear spectacles. It prevents your lenses from getting wet and also stops the sweat and hair from getting into your eyes while playing.

BADMINTON EQUIPMENTS : SHUTTLECOCK, RACKETS, SHOES, STRING, AND CLOTHING

The indispensable equipments for badminton are racket and shuttlecock. Sometimes beginners spend much on racket, thinking they can play well if their materials are expensive. In fact, the equipments that need to be well made are shoes, string, grip, racket, and at last but not least, clothing.

Here are some of the tips that players need to consider in choosing those equipment.

How to Choose Shuttlecock or Birdie

Choose shuttlecock according to your playing level and your wallet.

Nylon Shuttlecock

If you are a beginner or just want to play recreationally, you can start from plastic/nylon shuttlecock. It will save you more money because it is 2 to 4 times more durable than feather shuttlecock.

The recommended brand sfor nylon shuttlecock are :

Yonex Marvis 350 or higher quality Yonex Marvis 2000. There is a model called Ashaway Bird 2 that many people say that it is the best for nylon shuttlecock. People say Ashaway Bird 2 is almost similar to feather shuttlecock. Unfortunately it is quite difficult to get.

The feel of hitting the nylon shuttlecock will differ much from hitting feather shuttlecock. The flight and feel of nylon shuttlecock is different from feather shuttlecock.

If you want to play in real sport or competition, train with feather shuttlecock. It is different.

There are various speed of nylon shuttlecock to choose from according to temperature and your altitude.

Speed level for Yonex nylon shuttlecock:

- Green Label has slow speed level for use in 22-32 Celsius 71.6 – 89.6 Fahrenheit
- Blue Label has medium speed level for use in 12-23 Celsius 53.6- 73.4 Fahrenheit
- Red Label has fast speed level for use in 0- 13 Celsius or 32- 55.4 Fahrenheit

Feather Shuttlecock

Feather shuttlecock come in two materials, duck feather or goose feather. Goose feather has better quality.

The best shuttlecock according to many player is Yonex Aerosense 50 but it can cost US$ 30 for a tube of 12 pcs.

Good brands of shuttlecock are Yonex, Victor, Aerosense, RCL, Lining, RSL, Protech, and Youhe.

You can look at the list below for badminton shuttlecocks that are approved in international tournament. This is the Badminton World Federetion approved list of shuttlecock as of 2015.

- PROTECH MASTERPIECE
- BABOLAT TOUR COMPETITION

- RSL Classic Tourney
- CARLTON GT1
- FLEET NO. 2002
- FZ FORZA VIP
- JINQUE AAA
- LI-NING A+600 INTERNATIONAL TOURNAMENT
- YOUHE S100
- YANG YANG 300B TOURNAMENT GRADE
- SNOWPEAK SUPERIOR SP101
- VICTOR MASTER ACE
- WILSON TOUR 100 FOR TOURNAMENT GRADE
- YONEX AEROSENSA 40 AS-40
- YONEX AEROSENSA 50 AS-50
- YONEX TOURNAMENT F-90
- YONEX SHUTTLECOCK AEROCLUB 33 (ACB-33)

Badminton Feather Shuttlecock Speed

There is speed-type shuttlecock that determines how far and fast the shuttlecock will travel. Shuttlecock speeds is to be chosen differently for each season and region of play. For example, shuttles with Speed 76 are used in China during the summer and 77 during the winter months. Speed 76 or 77 for Singapore. Speed 77 or 78 for United States.

1	48	75	slow, for use in highland
2	49	76	slow, medium slow, for use in hotter area
3	50	77	slow, medium, most sea level area
4	51	78	slow, medium fast, cold area
5	52	79	slow, fast, cold area, below sea level

Yonex has chart for their shuttlecock choices. It is according to the temperature.

In tournament, they will test three shuttle speed. International tournament will use shuttlecock speed that pass the speed test according to Badminton World Federation's Laws.

How to Increase the Durability of Shuttlecock

In order to save the durability of shuttlecock, steam the shuttlecock 1-2 days prior to using it. Or you can try to put it in your shower room when you use hot water so it get the moisture from the steam. But don't wet it.

How to Choose Badminton Racket

The biggest factor when deciding which racket to use is your playing style and experience.

There are rackets that excel for offense but on the other hand are not very fast in defense. Some rackets are good for defense but not good for attack. It is a trade-off.

For beginners and recreational playing, choose any cheap decent badminton racket. You could buy other brands than Yonex like Apacs or Victor because usually you need to pay more for Yonex low-end racket than if you buy others decent brands of the same quality. I cannot give any recommendation because the availability of the racket and pricing is different in each country..

Brands for rackets include Yonex, Apacs, Victor, Lining, RSL, etc You will need to understand the terminology to understand which racket is best suited for you. Terminology to understand.

Weight

It is the weight of the racket denoted by U. Bigger number means lighter weight.

U = 95-100g, 2U = 90-94g, 3U = 85-89g, 4U = 80-84g

For beginner, use light racket.

Lightest racket is not equivalent to best racket. Lighter racket gives more maneuverability and faster swing. On the other hand, heavier racket gives more stability and more power in shooting.

Grip

The grip size is denoted by "G"; Bigger number means smaller handlesize.

Just choose according to your hand size, not too big and not too small.

Shaft Flexibility

Stiff or flexible. It determines how flexible the shaft when you swing the racket. For beginner with slow swing speed, use flexible shaft. As you becomes more experienced and stronger, your swing will be faster. At that time, you could use stiffer shaft racket.

Flexible shaft racket is not suitable for short and explosive swing . Flexible shaft needs time to flex first, so when you swing it fast with short swing, the shaft will not react in time to transfer the energy. Using flexible shaft racket with short and explosive swing will make you miss the shuttlecock and result in lack of shooting power .

Stiff shaft racket is suited for short and explosive swing. So choose the shaft flexibility according to your hitting style.

Oval or Isometric Head

Oval is the traditional head shape. Oval rackets have a small but more concentrated sweet spot. The isometric head has a wider and more squared top half of the racket head. It has a larger sweet spot so easier to hit the shuttlecock.

Balance Point

The point on the racket's shaft where it can be balanced, is measured from the end of the handle to the balance point. Head-heavy means, it is heavier in the head side. Head-light means it is heavier in the handle side.

Use head-light racket for defensive style especially when playing around the net in double play. Head-light racket is better in maneuverability so it is better when you need to react quickly.

A head-heavy racket is suited for attack style players looking for extra power on their shots.

How to Choose Shoes

Shoes is the most important equipment in playing badminton. You can have a bad racket to play but later you can change it. You need a good shoes from the start to prevent you from injury and give your knees and ankle better support. You can buy racket with money but you can't buy your health with money. Running shoes is not suitable for playing.

The best brands for shoes are Victor and Yonex. Recently, there are many good reviews for Victor badminton shoes. Choose their badminton shoes or other brands according to your budget.

You can put additional insole in your shoes for additional support. Many people give good reviews for Spenco Total Support insole, available in thin, original, and max.

How to Choose Grip Tape

Grip tape is important because your hand will always be in contact with the grip tape when holding the racket. Grip tape is to absorb the shock in the hand and to absorb the sweat keeping your hand dry.

Choose the grip tape according to your preference. Things to keep in mind, grip size will change with grip tape that you choose.

There are towel type and synthetic type grip. Towel type is better in absorbing sweat but more prone to germ. Synthetic type is not germ-prone but not as good as towel type in absorbing sweat. Choose according to your preference.

How to Choose Badminton String

Use proper tension according to your skill level. Higher tension reward strong hit with stronger power, but power of lighter hit will decrease. Lower tension reward light hit but not as good for strong hit .

Here is the recommended tension for string according to skill level.

- Beginners: 19-20lbs
- Intermediate players: 21-24lbs
- Advance players: 25+ lbs.

How to Choose Badminton Set

Badminton set is available for recreational play because it is cheaper. Usually the set includes two badminton rackets, and a shuttlecock. It is suitable for people that just want to play for fun and never want to play it competitively.

Usually it is very cheap so the quality of the racket and shuttlecock is not suitable for competitive play. You can find it in many places. Yonex sells some badminton set too. You can save money using the set if you just want to play for fun.

Clothing

Use light and nonrestrictive clothing. Clothing that restricts your hand movement is not suitable for playing. Shorts is the preference for players because it allows easier feet movement.

Playing badminton will make you sweat a lot so use clothing that suitable for sweat.

Just keep that things in your mind when choosing your clothing.

Those are tips to guide you when choosing your equipments. Although equipment is important, your playing skill is the most important things to improve.

RACKET (SPORTS EQUIPMENT)

A racket or racquet is a sports implement consisting of a handled frame with an open hoop across which a network of strings or catgut is stretched tightly. It is used for striking a ball or shuttlecock in games such as squash, tennis, racquetball, and badminton. Collectively, these games are known as racket sports. This predecessor to the modern game of squash, rackets, is played with 30 D_2-inch-long (77 cm) wooden rackets. While squash equipment has evolved in the intervening century, rackets equipment has changed little.

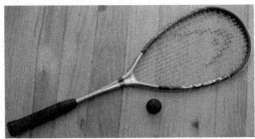

The frame of rackets for all sports was traditionally made of laminated wood and the strings of animal intestine known as catgut. The traditional racket size was limited by the strength and weight of the wooden frame which had to be strong enough to hold the strings and stiff enough to hit the ball or shuttle. Manufacturers started adding non-wood laminates to wood rackets to improve stiffness. Non-wood rackets were made first of steel, then of aluminium, and then carbon fiber composites. Wood is still used for real tennis, rackets, and xare. Most rackets are now made of composite materials including carbon fiber or fiberglass, metals such as titanium alloys, or ceramics. Catgut has partially been replaced by synthetic materials including nylon, polyamide, and other polymers. Rackets are restrung when necessary, which may be after every match for a professional. Despite the name, "catgut" has never been made from any part of a cat.

Spelling

Racket is the standard spelling of the word. *Racquet* is an alternative spelling used more commonly in certain sports (squash, racquetball, badminton) and less commonly in others (tennis). While some writers, especially those outside North America, prefer the French-influenced *racquet*, *racket* is the predominant spelling by a large margin. Similarly, while some believe that *racket* came about as a misspelling of *racquet*, *racket* is in fact the older spelling: it has been in use since the 16th century, with *racquet* only showing up later in the 19th century as a variant of *racket*.

Etymology

The origin of the term "racket" is unclear. According to a popular belief first published by Malcolm Whitman in 1932, the expression comes from the Arabic term *rahat al-yad*, meaning "palm of hand". Modern research however, holds this thesis in a highly questionable light. Instead, the term is more likely to be derived from the Flemish word "raketsen" which is itself derived from Middle French "rachasser", meaning "to strike (the ball) back".

Badminton

Badminton rackets are light, with top quality rackets weighing between about 70 and 95 grams (with guts). Modern rackets are composed of carbon fiber composite (graphite reinforced plastic), which may be augmented by a variety of materials. Carbon fiber has an excellent strength to weight ratio, is stiff, and gives excellent kinetic energy transfer. Before the adoption of carbon fibre composite, rackets were made of wood to their excessive weight and cost. There is a wide variety of racket designs, although the racket size and shape are limited by the Laws. Different rackets have playing characteristics that appeal to different players. The traditional oval head shape is still available, but an isometric head shape is increasingly common in new rackets. Various companies have emerged but Yonex of Japan and Li-Ning of China are the dominant players in the market. The majority of top tournaments are sponsored by these companies. Every year a new technology is introduced by these companies but predominantly, all rackets are made of carbon graphite composite.

They have another quality like reflex which differ from 6to8 in low quality an 8 to 12or13 in good quality.For good quality of guts or stings as people say li-ning and yonex bg5,65 are best guts guts for a good racket.

Rackets

This predecessor to the modern game of squash, rackets, is played with 30 D$_2$-inch (770 mm) wooden rackets. While squash equipment has evolved in the intervening century, rackets equipment has changed little.

Racquetball

According to the current racquetball rules there are no limitations on the weight of a racquetball racket.

1. The racket, including bumper guard and all solid parts of the handle, may not exceed 22 inches in length.
2. The racket frame may be any material judged safe.
3. The racket frame must include a cord that must be securely attached to the player's wrist.
4. The string of the racket must be gut, monofilament, nylon, graphite, plastic, metal, or a combination thereof, and must not mark or deface the ball.
5. Using an illegal racket will result in forfeiture of the game in progress or, if discovered between games, forfeiture of the preceding game.

Racquetball rackets, unlike many other types, generally have little or no neck, the grip connecting directly to the head. They also tend to have head shapes that are notably wider at the top, with some older rackets looking almost triangular or teardrop shaped.

Real tennis

Real tennis rackets and balls: In real tennis, 27-inch (686-mm) long rackets are made of wood and very tight strings to cope with the game's heavy balls. The racket heads are bent slightly to make striking balls close to the floor or in corners easier.

Squash

Standard squash rackets are governed by the rules of the game. Traditionally they were made of laminated timber (typically Ash), with a small strung area using natural gut strings. After a rule change in the mid-1980s, they are now almost always made of composite materials such as carbon fiber or metals (graphite, Kevlar, titanium, and/or boron) with synthetic strings. Modern rackets are 70 cm long, with a maximum strung area of 500 square centimetres (approximately 75 square inches) and a mass between 90 and 200 grams (4–7 ounces).

Table tennis

Table Tennis racket with 3 different sizes of the celluloid ball.

Table tennis uses a table tennis racket made from laminated wood covered with rubber on one or two sides depending on the grip of the player. Unlike a conventional racket, it does not contain strings strung across an open frame. This is called either a paddle, racket, or a bat, with usage differing by region. In the USA the term "paddle" is common, in Europe the term is "bat", and the official ITTF term is "racket."

Table Tennis racket specs are defined at the ITTF handbook section 2.04 and currently include the following.

2.04.01: The racket may be of any size, shape or weight but the blade shall be flat and rigid.

2.04.02: At least 85% of the blade by thickness shall be of natural wood; an adhesive layer within the blade may be reinforced with fibrous material such as carbon fibre, glass fibre or compressed paper, but shall not be thicker than 7.5% of the total thickness or 0.35mm, whichever is the smaller.

2.04.03: A side of the blade used for striking the ball shall be covered with either ordinary pimpled rubber, with pimples outwards having a total thickness including adhesive of not more than 2.0mm, or sandwich rubber, with pimples inwards or outwards, having a total thickness including adhesive of not more than 4.0mm.

2.04.03.01: *Ordinary pimpled rubber* is a single layer of non-cellular rubber, natural or synthetic, with pimples evenly distributed over its surface at a density of not less than 10 per cm and not more than 30 per cm.

2.04.03.02: *Sandwich rubber* is a single layer of cellular rubber covered with a single outer layer of ordinary pimpled rubber, the thickness of the pimpled rubber not being more than 2.0mm.

2.04.04: The covering material shall extend up to but not beyond the limits of the blade, except that the part nearest the handle and gripped by the fingers may be left uncovered or covered with any material.

2.04.05: The blade, any layer within the blade and any layer of covering material or adhesive on a side used for striking the ball shall be continuous and of even thickness.

2.04.06: The surface of the covering material on a side of the blade, or of a side of the blade if it is left uncovered, shall be matt, bright red on one side and black on the other.

2.04.07: The racket covering shall be used without any physical, chemical or other treatment.

2.04.07.01: Slight deviations from continuity of surface or uniformity of colour due to accidental damage or wear may be allowed provided that they do not significantly change the characteristics of the surface.

2.04.08: Before the start of a match and whenever he or she changes his or her racket during a match a player shall show his or her opponent and the umpire the racket he or she is about to use and shall allow them to examine it.

Tennis

A modern tennis racket, with carbon fiber-reinforced polymer frame.

Currently-popular lawn tennis rackets vary primarily in length, weight, balance point, stiffness, beam thickness, string pattern, string density, and head size. They also conform to some unofficial standards that differ from racquets now considered obsolete. For instance, all racquets for serious play made today are made from graphite composite, not wood, steel, fiberglass, aluminum, or other materials. This comes despite the fact that those other materials are legal for play. Very inexpensive discount racquets, which have poor performance characteristics, such as excessive flexibility and inadequate weight, may still be made from aluminum. No racquets of recent times use single-throated beams. Prince tried to reintroduce the single throat design in the 1990s but the only professional who used one was Mirjana Luèiæ. Braided graphite racquets have found very serious use, mainly in the past, but molded racquets have been the norm for a long time. They are less expensive to manufacture and offer higher stiffness. Dunlop also had a nylon-based "hot melt" process, now obsolete, that produced the midsize 200G racquet, once used to great effect by Steffi Graf and John McEnroe, as well as briefly used by Martina Navratilova.

For length, 21 to 26 inches (53 to 66 cm) is normally the junior racquet range, while 27 inches (69 cm) is for stronger more physically-mature players. Some are also available at lengths of 27.5 to 29 inches (70 to 74 cm). The Gamma Big Bubba was produced with a 32 inches (81 cm) length but it is no longer legal in that length. Gamma responded by changing the length of the grip portion of the racquet, to continue sales. The length restriction was based on the concern that such long racquets would make the serve too dominant, but that concern has never been objectively supported with testing. Moreover, some players, such as John Isner, are much taller and have longer arms than average professionals (and especially low stature ones), giving them a much larger advantage in terms of height for the service than is possible with several inches of racquet length. This makes the length restriction more questionable. Finally, the professionals who nearly always choose to use the longest racquets typically choose them because they use two-handed groundstrokes for both forehand and backhand, using the extra length to improve their reach. An example is Marion Bartoli. As this type of player is not dominant in the sport, or even close to being average in terms of per capita representation, the length restriction seems even more unnecessary. Despite Prince's attempt to market longer length "longbody" racquets in the 1990s, standard length remains the overwhelming choice of players, further negating the argument in favor of the length restriction. When most players who choose to use a longer racquet than 27 inches (69 cm) choose one, they typically only use a 27.5 inches (70 cm) model, rather than one approaching 30 inches (76 cm). Longer rackets were introduced by Dunlop

Weights of a racket also vary between 7 ounces (200 g) unstrung and 12.6 ounces (360 g) strung. Until the 1980s, racquets weighted at "medium" were produced. "Heavy" racquets were produced during the height of the wood era (e.g. the 1960s), very sparingly. The "medium" weight is heavier than any of the racquets produced since it was discontinued by companies. Many professionals added weight to their racquets to improve stability. Many continue to do so. Pete Sampras added lead tape to make his racquet have a 14 ounces (400 g) weight and Venus Williams is known for using a frame modified to be quite heavy, in terms of the recent times average. By contrast, Andy Roddick surprised many when he said he used a stock Pro Drive series model, series of racquet which was light when compared with the racquets used by most top professionals. In both recreational and professional tennis, the trend has been away from heavy racquets and toward lighter racquets, despite the drawbacks from light racquets, such as increased twisting. Lawn tennis rackets originally flared outward at the bottom of the handle to prevent slippage. The rounded bottom was called a bark bottom after its inventor Matthew Barker. But by 1947, this style became superfluous. More mass gives racquets "plow through", momentum that continues once the player has managed to get the racquet into motion and which is more resistant to stoppage from the ball's momentum. This can give the perception that the racquet produces shots with more power, although this is complicated by the typically slower stroke production. Higher mass typically involves a slower swing but more energy to execute the swing.

More mass also provides more cushioning against ball impact shock, a source of injuries such as tennis elbow. However, high racquet mass can cause fatigue in the shoulder area. Typically, it is safer for the body to have higher mass. More mass, additionally, provides more stability. It makes the racquet more resistant to twisting forces and pushback. The drawbacks are that heavier racquets have lower maneuverability (reducing reaction time) and require more energy to move. As a racquet gets heavier, the player finds it increasingly difficult to do fast reaction shots such as quick volleys and returns of serve. However, the additional mass can help with return of serve, in particular, by making the racquet much more resistant to twist from a high-powered service. Light racquets have the additional drawback of making it easier for beginning players to use inappropriate wrist-dominant strokes, which often leads to injury. This is because poor stroke mechanics can be much easier to produce with a lightweight racquet, such as in using one's wrist to mostly swing the racquet. An extremely typical mistake beginning players make is to choke up heavily on the racquet (to try to compensate for twist from a light racquet, as well as too high racquet angle upon impact) and use the wrist too much. The only professional well-known player to have had success with a strongly choked-up grip is Zina Garrison.

Head size plays a very key role in a racket's performance characteristics. A larger head size very generally means more power and a larger "sweet spot". This is an area in the string bed that is partially more forgiving on off-center hits and which produces more ball-reflective power from string deformation, known as the trampoline effect. However, large head sizes can increase twisting, which makes off-center hits more difficult to control and can reduce a player's overall power production due to the playing compensating for the extra inherent power, typically with stiffer strings to reduce the increased string deformation of large heads. A smaller head size generally offers more control for many shots, particularly the service and groundstrokes aimed near the lines, but can lead to more shanks (wild misses, from hitting the frame or missing the sweet spot). This drawback is most common for professional players using single-handed topspin backhands, as well as for recreational and aged players at net. Shanking due to small racquet head size is typically exacerbated by racquet weight, which slows the reaction time, as well as, to a lesser degree, the racquet's balance point.

In professional tennis, currently-used racket head sizes vary between 95–115 square inches (610–740 cm), with most players adopting one from 98–108 square inches (630–700 cm). Racquets with smaller and larger head sizes, 85 and 120–137 square inches (550 and 770–880 cm), are still produced but are not used by professionals currently. A very small number of professionals, such as Monica Seles, used 125 square inches (810 cm) racquets during some point in their careers. Racquets with smaller heads than 85 square inches (550 cm) have not been in production since the 1980s and racquets with larger head sizes than 137 square inches (880 cm) are not currently legal for the sport, even though only elderly players typically choose to use racquets beyond 115 square inches (740 cm) and it is nearly unheard-of for a serious player who is not elderly to choose a racquet over 125 square inches (810 cm).

The WEED company, founded by Tad Weed, specializes in producing very large racquets, primarily for the elderly market. Rackets that are moderately higher in power production, moderately lower in weight, moderately larger in size, and which typically possess a slightly head-heavy balance are often called *"tweener rackets."* Racquets that have the smallest heads in current use, the highest weights in current use, and headlight or even balance are referred to as "players' racquets". Oversize racquets, typically 110 square inches (710 cm) in size, were once pejoratively referred to as "granny sticks" but resistance to them being seen as illegitimate racquets for younger players decreased dramatically with the successful use of these racquets by a small number professionals such as Andrei Agassi and Pam Shriver. Originally, even midsize frames (85 square inches (550 cm)) were considered jumbo, and some top players, such as Martina Navratilova and Rod Laver said they should be banned for making the sport too easy. Later, these same professionals, including John McEnroe, signed a letter supporting a switch back to wood frames, or a limitation to the original standard size of approximately 65 square inches (420 cm). Perhaps the last professional to use a standard-size racquet in professional tennis was Aaron Krickstein, known for the strongly-contested match against Connors at the 1991 US Open. He used a Wilson Ultra-II standard-size graphite racquet also used in the 1980s by the hard-hitting teen Andrea Jaeger. The first oversize, the fiberglass Bentley Fortissimo from Germany, was praised by racquet designers but was considered too large to be taken seriously by the small number of players who were exposed to it.

One of the ways a tennis racket can be held. The head-light balance point is rarer in professional tennis than it once was, as the sport has converted to larger-headed racquets, stiffer racquets, stiffer strings, more western grips and accompanying stroke production, and more topspin. The head-light balance point is most optimal for the serve and volley style with a continental grip. Serve and volley is no longer a viable option for nearly all professionals as the mode of playing for most points in a match. Head-heavy racquets became popular, mainly with recreational players, primarily with the introduction of the Wilson ProFile widebody racquet. The head-light balance makes volleys and serves easier to produce, while groundstrokes are less stable. The head-heavy balance makes groundstrokes more stable, which typically increases the player's comfort for swinging harder to add power, but makes serves and volleys more cumbersome. A head-heavy balance also puts more stress on the elbow and shoulder.

Vibration dampeners (also sometimes known as "gummies") may be interlaced in the proximal part of the string array, to reduce the percussive sound of the ball hitting the strings and/ or to reduce perceived vibration. They do not, however, reduce impact shock significantly, so they are of no safety value. Some professionals, such as Andrei Agassi, used rubber bands instead of specialized dampeners. Dampeners come in two main types.

The first uses the two central main strings to hold it in place. The second is sometimes called a "worm" and it is woven between many of the main strings. Dampeners are nearly always placed very near the bottom of the racquet string bed.

As racquets have become lighter, stiffer, and larger-headed, the professional game has moved, basically completely, from softer and more flexible string materials to stiff materials. This is, in large part, to tone down the additional power potential of the "modern" racquets. However, it also is related to the tendency for different string materials to move out of place when subjected to heavy topspin strokes. Polyester is the string of choice today because of that resistance, despite its increased stiffness (harsher feel and more aggravating for the joints) and reduced tension-holding ability (versus a string like natural gut, which excels at that). The top professionals of the 1970s and earlier, despite having access to stiffer materials such as nylon, nearly always chose to use the very flexible natural gut instead. String bed stiffness can be increased by using stiffer materials, such as kevlar and polyester, by increasing the density of the string pattern, and by stringing with a higher tension. Racquet makers and players have experimented with very dense string patterns and very "open" patterns, beginning with the Snauwaert Hi Ten, which had a pattern with as few as 12 mains and 13 crosses. Doubles great Mark Woodforde used one of them. More recently, Grigor Dimitrov is known for having played with a very open-patterned racquet during part of his career. String choice, both in thickness and material, string tension, string pattern, and string pattern density can have a very large effect on how a racquet performs.

Throughout most of lawn tennis' history, most rackets were made of laminated wood, with heads of around 65 square inches (420 cm). A small number of them were made of metal, such as a 1920s racquet by Dayton. Some, rarely, also had metal strings. In the late 1960s, Wilson popularized the T-2000 steel racket with wire wound around the frame to make string loops, after having purchased the design from René Lacoste, who produced the racquet first in a more limited run. It was popularized by the top American player Jimmy Connors and was also, prior to Connors using it, by Billie Jean King in her early career. Many players said it lacked control but had more power, when compared with wood frames of the period. Connors used the rarer "firm" model that had additional throat welds to increase its stiffness. In 1968 Spalding launched an aluminum racket, called The Smasher. Aluminum, though lighter and more flexible than steel, was sometimes less accurate than wood. The biggest complaint, however, was that metal racquets caused strong cases of tennis elbow, especially the kind that had holes for the strings directly in the frame, rather than using an external wire wrapper, as in the T-2000. Because of that drawback in particular, most of the top players still preferred to use wooden frames.

By 1975, aluminum construction improvements allowed for the introduction of the first American "oversized" racket, which was manufactured by Weed. Prince popularized the oversize racket, which had a head size of approximately 110 square inches (710 cm). Howard Head was able to obtain a broad patent for Prince, despite the prior art of the Bentley Fortissimo (the first oversize, made in Germany of fiberglass) and the Weed. The patent was rejected by Germany but approved in the USA. The popularity of the Prince aluminum oversize had the side effect of popularizing rackets having other non-standard head sizes such as mid-size 85–90 square inches (550–580 cm) and mid-plus sizes 95–98 square inches (610–630 cm). Fairly quickly, midsize frames began to become the most-used frames in the pro tours. Ironically, Martina Navratilova popularized the midsize graphite racquet, with her wins using the Yonex R-7, the first midsize graphite racquet made by Yonex. Nearly at the same time, however, she said the "jumbo" racquets (midsize included) should be removed from the sport for making it easier. She said she would use them only because other players could, as they were tournament-legal. Fewer players chose to use oversize racquets, and some switched to midplus frames after their earliest career for more control. Fiberglass frames also had a brief period of limited popularity, making fewer inroads among top players than aluminum. Also, the earliest composites, such as the Head Competition series, used by Arthur Ashe, were made without graphite. These were more flexible than a typical early graphite composite but stiffer than wood, fiberglass, and aluminum.

In the early 1980s, "graphite" (carbon fibre) composites were introduced, and other materials were added to the composite, including ceramics, glass fibre, boron, and titanium. Some of the earliest models typically had 20% or more fiberglass, to make them more flexible. Stiff racquets were typically not preferred by most players because of their familiarity with the comfortable softness of wood. These early models tended to be very flexible and not very powerful, although they were a power upgrade over wood and metal racquets. Wilson created the Jack Kramer Pro Staff, the graphite version of the extremely popular wood racquet of the same name, which was the origin of the extremely influential Wilson Pro Staff 85. Chris Evert's first graphite racquet was this Jack Kramer version, which had 20% fiberglass. It was not a market success and she, along with everyone else, quickly replaced it with the stiffer Pro Staff 85, which had 20% kevlar. It used the same mold and had the same braided graphite, but offered a very noticeable improvement in power. The very popular Prince original graphite, an oversize in its most popular form, was also quite influential and used by many pros, especially as juniors. Jennifer Capriati and Monica Seles, for instance, used the Prince graphite to contest their influential Wimbledon match in 1991 that has often been hailed as the beginning of the power baselining game in the WTA, although that claim is somewhat hyperbolic and is, in large part, due to the mistaken impression that the players were hitting much harder when, in fact, the racquets were more powerful. However, the very large head size, when compared with the midsize and, especially, the old "standard" size, made it easier to produce power. The racquet also had an open string pattern. The Prince "original" graphite name is rather a misnomer, as it went through some significant design adjustments over its lifetime. For instance, the truly original model had a reverse teardrop head shape, something no subsequent versions had. Stiffer composite rackets, when compared with the first and second generations of graphite composites, are the contemporary standard.

A United States tennis racket from the 1970s

The last wooden racquet appearing at Wimbledon appeared in 1987, long after they were abandoned by practically all professionals. Borg tried to stage a comeback with his standard wood racquet, after his premature retirement, but it quickly ended in failure, as the standard wood was no match when placed against a stiff midplus graphite. It is also commonly argued that Chris Evert would have been able to beat Martina Navratilova during the latter's most dominant period if she had switched from her wood racquet years sooner. Additionally, the last influential wooden racquet, the Prince Woodie, had layers of graphite to increase its stiffness and was an oversize. It was used by Tommy Haas, Gabriela Sabatini, and quite a few others. It offered very little power but did offer much more surface area than a standard-size wooden frame. Sabatini found it helpful, as compared with smaller racquets, due to her production of heavy topspin. The only woman to beat Martina

Navratilova in 1984, Kathleen Horvath, used the Prince Woodie, one of only six losses Navratilova suffered in a three-year stretch involving 260 matches.

A denser pattern is often considered to deliver more control, at the expense of spin potential. A more open pattern is often believed to offer greater potential for power and spin. However, how much power is produced by a player can be strongly influenced by how a player adapts to the characteristics of the racquet. Some players may hit harder with a dense string pattern, producing faster shots because of the added control from the dense pattern. Rackets, including those of much of the wood era, are marked with a recommended string tension range. The basic rule is that a lower tension creates more power (from the trampoline effect) and a higher string tension creates more control (less string deformation which results in a more predictable the power and angle of the departure from the string bed.)

Some professionals used small-headed racquets with flexible-material strings (natural gut) strung at very high tension. Examples include Pete Sampras and Björn Borg. Some used large-headed racquets with very inflexible-material strings (kevlar). Andrei Agassi is an example. Many professionals during the standard wood era strung at relatively low tension and used natural gut string; both decisions were to increase the trampoline effect for more power.

By contrast, almost every professional player today uses the much stiffer polyester string in their much stiffer racquets which also have larger heads and which tend to be lighter. Madeline Hauptman sold a line of racquets, called the MAD RAQ, which featured a Star of David pattern (a six-pointed figure consisting of two interlaced equilateral triangles), as it used three strings instead of two for stringing the racquet. This pattern is used in snowshoes. This stringing pattern was said to feature less string notching, improving string lifespan. It was even claimed that many pro shops refused to carry the racquet because less string breakage would reduce string and stringing service sales. It has also been claimed that the racquet is more difficult to string than a two string racquet. However, the Wilson T-2000-type requires a great deal more time for stringing than a typical racquet and racquets of that series were very popular. Whatever the cause of the failure of the MAD RAQ in the marketplace, it was the only time a snowshoe pattern was used in tennis. Hauptman switched her racquet line to a two string diamond pattern (PowerAngle). This pattern had already been used in much earlier racquets but had not had much popularity. It is said to be easier to string than the MAD RAQ but does not have the benefit of reduced string notching, at least not to the same degree. The claim is that this diagonal pattern offers more comfort than a traditional square pattern.

The stiffest graphite racquet that has been sold is the Prince More Game MP, which is rated at 80 RA on the industry-standard Babolat measuring equipment. The Prince More series used two pieces (a top side and bottom side of the racquet, or a left side and a right side) and no grommet strip. Interestingly, Prince had briefly used a design without a grommet strip in an early version of its "original" graphite oversize. The most famous user of a More series racquet was Martina Navratilova, who returned to play doubles in her 40s, using a Prince More Control DB (a midplus) for her initial wins in the mixed doubles at Wimbledon and the Australian Open with Leander Paes. She had used the stiffer More Game MP prior. Navratilova later switched to a design by Warren Bosworth (the founder of Bosworth Tennis) which had a customized asymmetric grip and an unusual geometric head shape. Stiffer racquets typically offer more power and control at the expense of increased ball shock, which can lead to injury or tennis elbow aggravation. Typically, power and control are at odds. However, in the case of stiff racquets, less energy is dissipated by the racquet deforming, transmitting it back to the ball. Control is improved because there is less deformation. However, a player's overall power level may decrease due to the need to moderate ball striking effort to reduce discomfort and even injury. Although known as a hard hitter in her younger years, in her 40s she was known more as a precision player who used finesse (and especially tactics) more than power. In fact, the last doubles partner she won a major with in mixed, Bob Bryan, remarked on how slow her serve was, despite how effective she was on the court. Navratilova also used string that was much softer than what anyone else on tour used (thick uncoated natural gut), to help compensate for the stiffness of her racquet. The vastly higher injury rate in tennis (when compared with the wood era) is, in part, due to the increase in stiffness, both of the racquet and of the strings.

Real tennis uses wooden racquets and cork-filled balls. It is a very different sport from today's lawn tennis.

BADMINTON FOOTWEAR & CLOTHING

To prevent injury and optimise performance, it is important to wear a pair of specific badminton shoes. Playing badminton involves a great deal of twisting and turning, often at high speed, and can be fairly vigorous on your knee and ankle joints. To reduce the risk of injury, it is important to wear a pair of shoes with very good grip, cushioning and also support for your ankles. It is also important that you find a pair which are comfortable!

Footwear

It is also worth taking steps to increase the lifespan of your badminton shoes. Once the cushioning is lost from the shoe, its protection and effectiveness is lessened, and thus injuries are more likely. Firstly, try and only wear your them for playing badminton or other indoor activities - don't go jogging in them! This will help them keep grip, and stop you slipping around the court. It is also worth replacing your in-soles if you feel the cushioning effect start to weaken!

Badminton Clothing

The most important thing regarding badminton clothing is comfort. Generally speaking there are no strict rules about what you can or cannot wear, but you are more likely to play well when wearing something comfortable and not overly restrictive. The majority of players will tend to wear a polo shirt or t-shirt and a pair of shorts or skirt. It is a bad idea to wear jeans or other restrictive trousers to play in!

BADMINTON RACKETS

A badminton racket is a pivotal piece of kit for all players. Whether you own one or borrow one, it is impossible to play a game without it! Trying to find the right racket can be a very confusing and daunting experience for even the most experienced of players. Here, we will try and give you a bit of information to make this experience as hassle free as possible!

Choosing a Badminton Racket

The age old question of 'which racket is best for me?' has been asked by many a badminton player around the globe. Choosing one can be an important decision for any aspiring player looking to perfect their game. Rackets come in all different shapes and colours, and at vastly differing prices, and it is impossible to give a generic answer as to which is the best. A racket which suits one person may not suit another, and vice-versa, as we are all unique with particular playing styles and preferences.

There are a number of differences between badminton rackets. Slight variance in weight, balance, flexibility, grip size and string tension can all make a difference to the way a racket affects your game.

One of the key differences between badminton rackets is the material from which it is made. Nowadays they are made from a variety of different materials such as graphite, titanium, kevlar or carbon. Some make the racket 'stiffer' than others, and some will be more flexible. The weight is also particularly important. Some players will prefer a heavier racket, helping power shots, and others will prefer a lighter more maneuverable racket making fast short movements much easier. Typically, decent badminton rackets weigh between 80 and 100 grams. The balance, or distribution, of this weight across the racket can also be a factor. Some people will prefer a 'head-heavy' racket, and others 'head-light'.

Badminton Racket String Tension

How tightly to have your racket strung is another subjective matter. Modern day badminton rackets can withstand tensions up to about 30 lbs, however most players would not have it anywhere near this tight. Typically, players have rackets strung at around 18-23 lbs, although some top professionals would be nearer the 30 lb mark. It is a common misconception that the tighter you have it strung, the more power you get. In fact the opposite is true! Lower tensions give you more power, whereas higher tensions give a far greater level of control over the shuttle. String tension is another example of personal preference, but as a rule of thumb something around the 21 lb mark is common for most amateur players.

A plethora of manufacturers exist, all proclaiming that they make the best racket. The truth is that the most important thing is the racket itself, rather than any brand name. That said, here is some information on a few of the most popular brands, to help you make a more informed choice:

Yonex Badminton Rackets

Based in Tokyo, Japan, Yonex have become the most well-known brand in badminton. They have been exclusive sponsor to the 'All England Championships' for the past 15 years, and also have a strong presence in sports such as tennis and golf. Upwards of 80% of professional badminton players, including Peter Gade, Taufik Hidyat and Lee Choong Wei, use Yonex equipment.

Carlton Rackets

Based in the UK, Carlton have a very rich history in the sport. Carlton have been pioneers in badminton technology over the years, and can boast to be the first manufacturer to make all-metal rackets. Players such as Olympic silver medalist Nathan Robertson use Carlton equipment.

Wilson Rackets

Based in Chicago, USA, Wilson are one of the biggest sport manufacturers in the world. They also have a very strong presence in other sports such as American football, baseball and tennis. Players such as former World Champion and current European Champion in mens doubles, Jonas Rasmussen use Wilson badminton equipment.

Head Rackets

With a very rich history in tennis, Head are a relative newcomer to the badminton market. They are a popular brand and players such as England's Anthony Clark use their equipment.

The question - 'which racket is best for me?' - really is very subjective. Most lower end rackets are fairly all-covering, and will offer more forgiveness to the badminton beginner. With the more high-end products it really is a case of trial and error- but with vast rewards if you find the optimum racket which suits your game. There is a racket out there for everybody - its just a case of finding it!

6

Scoring System Development of Badminton

Various scoring systems in badminton were developed during the sport's history. Since 2006, international competition uses the 3 x 21 rally point system as endorsed by the Badminton World Federation.

HOW TO PLAY BADMINTON?

Badminton is similar to other racket games, but it requires swift wrist and arm movements. The feathered shuttlecock has a greater aerodynamic drag and it swings differently from a ball. Below is a simplified version of badminton rules that can acclimatize you to the game.

Getting Ready and Serving

The game starts with a toss. The referee tosses the coin and one player calls 'Head' or 'Tail'. Player or team that wins the toss has an option to choose a side of the court, or an option to serve or receive first. If the player chooses his/her preferred side of the court then, the opponent player or team can choose to serve or receive first and vice versa.

Serving is done diagonally and the first serve is made from the right hand service court. The server should hit the shuttle underarm while it is below his/her waist. The server cannot step on boundaries and should serve from the correct service court. If the shuttle hits the net and doesn't cross it after the service, it has to be served again. If the server commits a fault while serving the opponent gets the opportunity to serve.

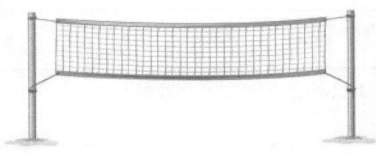

The receiving player receives the shuttlecock from the correct service court diagonally opposite to the server's court and returns it, thus starting a rally. Players can move around their side of the court after returning the service.

When a player shoots the shuttle outside the court boundaries or when a player misses to return the shuttle from his/her side of the court, the opponent gets a point and the rally ends. At the end of a game players change ends, and in a deciding game players change ends when one player or pair scores 8 (men) or 6 (ladies) points.

Serving rules for singles

The server serves from the right and left side of the service courts alternatively. Once the service is lost the opponent gets the chance.

If the players haven't scored any points or if they have scored an even number of points they serve from the right side of the service court to the right side of the opponent. If the players scored an odd number of points, they serve from the left side of the court to the left side of the opponent.

Serving rules for doubles

Each team gets two chances to serve, one for each player. The members in a team serve alternatively. After losing two serves the opposite team gets a chance to serve, and they start from the right side of the court.

The serving team gets only one chance to serve at the beginning of the game. In Doubles, the pair that served in the previous rally and at the receiving end in the current rally doesn't change their sides. Players that win a rally and are serving change their sides.

If the players haven't scored any points or if they have scored an even number of points they serve from the right side of the service court to the right side of the opponent. If the players scored an odd number of points, they serve from the left side of the court to the left side of the opponent.

Scoring

When the serving side wins a rally a point is added to its score and the player/team serves the next rally. When the receiving side wins a rally they add a point to their score and serve the next rally. A rally is won when a player or team makes a fault or when the shuttle lands in the opponent's court.

The most common faults during a rally are "

- Not hitting the shuttle before it lands within the boundaries.
- The shuttle is hit into the net.
- The shuttle fails to fly above the net.
- The shuttle lands outside the court boundary (if the shuttle lands on a line, it is in, but if a player steps on a line while serving or receiving, they are out)
- The player's body or the racket coming into contact with the net.
- Same player hitting the shuttle subsequently.

Winning a match

- The best of three games make a match.
- The team or player scoring 21 points faster, wins a game.
- If the score of both the teams is 20 (20-all), then the team that gets a 2 point lead wins the game.

- If the score of both the teams is 29 (29-all), then the team that reaches 30th point first wins the game.
- The winner of a game also wins the right to serve first in the next game.

Fouls

- Players should hit the shuttle only from their side of the court.
- Players should not touch the net or slide under it.
- The racket of a player should not land on the opposing team's side.
- The shuttle should never hit players, even outside the boundaries.
- In Doubles, the shuttle shouldn't hit a player or his clothing or his racket before his teammate hits it.
- Both feet of a player should be on the ground while serving and receiving the service.

ORIGINAL SYSTEM

The original scoring system in badminton dates back to as early as 1873. A match or rubber is decided by the best of three games. Each game is played to 15 points in the case of men's singles and any doubles games. In the case of ladies' singles, a game is played to 11 points.

The traditional scoring system also allows for a single game to determine a match or rubber. In this instance the game would be played to 21 points.

The first service is usually determined by the equivalent of a coin toss. Usually, the shuttle is dropped on top of the net; the server is appointed by the direction it points to when it falls to the floor. Thereafter a rally has to be won for service to change or a point to be won.

In singles, if the server loses a rally, the service would be transferred to the opponent. If the server wins a rally, their score is increased by one point. In doubles, if the server loses a rally, the service would transfer to their partner (except if serving first in the game) presenting a second opportunity to maintain scoring (second server).

If service is lost again, service is transferred to the opposition. If the server's team wins a rally, their team score is increased by one point.

In a game to 15 points, if the score reached 13–all, the player reaching 13 first would have the choice of "setting" or playing straight through to 15.

If they choose to "set", the score reverts to 0–0 and whoever scores five points wins the game. If the score reached 14–all, the player reaching 14 first would again have the option to "set" or play straight through to 15. This time however, the winner would be the first to score three points. In a game to 11 points, setting would occur at nine and 10 with "setting" to three and two points respectively. In a game to 21 points, setting would take place at 19 and 20 points "setting" to five and three respectively.

In 2002, "setting" at 13-13, 9–9 and 19–19 was dropped from the rules.

2002: scoring system—5 × 7

In 2002 the International Badminton Federation (BWF), concerned with the unpredictable and often lengthy time required for matches, decided to experiment with a different scoring system to improve the commercial and especially the broadcasting appeal of the sport. The new scoring system shortened games to seven points and decided matches by the best of five games. When the score reached 6–6, the player who first reached six could elect to set to eight points.

The match time remained an issue, since the playing time for the two scoring systems was similar. This experiment was abandoned and replaced by a modified version of the traditional scoring system. The 2002 Commonwealth Games was the last event that used this scoring system.

2005-2006: 3 × 21 rally point

In December 2005 the LBW experimented again with the scoring system, intending both to regulate the playing time and to simplify the system for television viewers. The main change from the traditional system was to adopt rally point scoring, in which the winner of a rally scores a point regardless of who served; games were lengthened to 21 points, with ladies' singles matches now using the same rules as men's singles. There must be at least a two point difference between scores.

In the old system, competitors may not be able to score after many exchanges, since serving is often slightly more difficult than defending, especially in professional badminton. Scoring is capped at 30 points, including the golden point rule at 29-all. In August 2006, the International Badminton Federation (now known as the Badminton World Federation (BWF)) adopted this system.

2014: experimental 5 × 11 rally point system

In the BWF Annual Grand Meeting in 2014 a review of the scoring system was performed. Match lengths had increased since the 2006 scoring system change. Several systems were considered in advance. In the end it was decided to try a system with 5 games to 11 points with no setting (i.e., the game ends no later then 11–10). The system will be tried during a period from August 1 to November 1, 2014 with certain tournaments using the new scoring system.

BADMINTON BASICS

If your conception of badminton is a quiet backyard barbecue game, you've never seen the pros in action. While this team sport is certainly quieter than bowling and less violent than football, players can work up quite a sweat. If it's a good aerobic workout you are looking for, step out onto the badminton court. Faster than a game of tennis, players can burn 600 to 1,000 calories an hour. We don't hear much about the sport of badminton in the United States, where sports coverage centers on baseball, basketball, football and hockey. But in Europe and Asia, professional badminton players get plenty of attention. In fact, in Indonesia, top badminton players take in the kind of money only players such as LeBron James and Derek Jeter earn here.

In any case, badminton is lots of fun and players with even a moderate amount of skill can jump right in and enjoy not only the social aspects of team play but also the fantastic health benefits of a great cardiovascular workout.

Badminton is played with a shuttlecock, also called a shuttle or bird, which is hit back and forth across a net by players using rackets.

Who can play?

The game of badminton is such a popular backyard party game because most novices find it very easy. You can take up the game as a small child or even well into your senior years because beginners can start with simple volleys back and forth and graduate to faster, more advance games as they refine their skills.

Dressing the part

Badminton players generally think about a few things when dressing for a game. You want to be able to move and lunge quickly, so try loose-fitting comfortable attire. Dressing the part sometimes helps to boost confidence so you may consider going to a sports clothing store where you can check out badminton outfits. If you are playing correctly, you will be perspiring a lot. Protect yourself in all types of weather by making sure your clothing easily absorbs sweat.

Professional badminton rules say that players must wear white, but for your backyard game, you could probably consider making this an option!

Badminton court and equipment

Along with the physical ability to run on the court and swing a racket, there are a few things you will need to play badminton. You need a badminton racket and a shuttlecock, which is a small rounded piece of cork or rubber with a conical crown of feathers or plastic. You'll also need a court and a net. You can play indoors if you want, but you'll need a high ceiling and proper lighting to assure that all players can see the shuttlecock sail through the air.

The court

The game can be played on a court that is any size and shape. (Professional badminton, however, is played on a court that measure 20 feet wide by 44 feet long.) A net or string (if you don't happen to have a net lying around) is placed 5 feet off the ground, spanning the width of the center of the court.

The racket

There are no specific rules governing the type or size of badminton racket that players can use for unofficial use. However, racket manufacturers have devised a standard: a racket of 26 inches in length and weighing 4.5 to 5.5 ounces.

While rackets used to be made of wood, most backyard models are made with metal and nylon. Many manufacturers make sets that include the net, racket and shuttlecocks so you can grab some teammates and get started.

How do you play badminton?

Similar to tennis, badminton is a racket sport for two or four players. Two people play a singles set while four players take to the court in teams of two for doubles play. The object of the game is to get to 21 points. Points are scored when the shuttlecock is successfully served or hit but not properly returned. The first team to win two matches wins the game.

Here are the basics of badminton play:

1. The first serve of the game is from the right half court to the half diagonally opposite.

2. If the receiving side commits a fault, the serving side gets a point and continues to serve.If the serving side commits a fault the receiving side gets a point.

3. In singles and in doubles the serve shifts to the opponent when a fault occurs.

4. In both singles and doubles, the serve is made alternately from the right half and the left half sides of the court.

5. Opponents change court ends after each game. The winning side serves first. A game consist of best of three, 21 points sets.

Badminton faults

There are three ways a player can cause a fault on the serve in the game of badminton. A fault occurs when the server a) strikes the shuttlecock at a point higher than the waist; b) holds the racket head higher than the hand; or c) fails to serve the shuttlecock in the proper court.

Other faults (loss of point or loss of serve) can occur during the rally. These faults occur when the shuttle: a) passes through or under the net; b) lands out of bounds; c) hits the ceiling or sidewalks; or d) the shuttlecock touches the clothing or body of a player.

Body language

The game of badminton is really a game of body language. The way a player grips the racket, moves around the court and shoots the shuttlecock can be the difference between winning and losing.

Gripping the racket: There are two basic grips from which all badminton shots are hit: the forehand and the backhand. When a player knows the difference between the shots, it's much easier to play and it's much easier to win!

For a right-handed forehand grip, take the racket in your left hand, holding it in front of you by the throat, parallel with the ground and with the strings perpendicular to the ground. Put the flat of your right hand against the strings, slide that hand down to the butt of the handle, and then close the fingers as though you are shaking hands with the handle. Handle and swing the racket as though it's an extension of your arms.

For the best backhand grip, take the correct forehand position with your arm extended. Bend your elbow so that your racket is across your body at the chest level with the strings perpendicular to the ground. Hold the racket firmly with your left hand and rotate your right hand toward your body until the thumb and the first finger "V" is in line with the two central main strings of the racket. Keeping your four fingers in place, move your thumb upward until it is on the handle and in line with those two middle strings.

Fancy footwork: While badminton is mainly an overhead game, a player has to know how to move on the court to get to the shuttlecock. Professional badminton players have what they call a "stance of readiness." From this stance, immediate movement in all directions is possible. The basic stance involves having your feet parallel and even with your shoulders. Point your toes toward the net, bend your knees slightly and keep you racket in your hand with your arm resting across the front of your body. Badminton players move around the court area in a series of fast moves including pushing off from the stance, a fast bouncing shuffle and a lunge, similar to a familiar fencer's move. From all of these positions, however, the player can easily bounce back into the "stance of readiness."

Striking the shuttle: The game of badminton includes a variety of strokes, some aimed at basic play and others used by advanced players. The main strokes, however, are done in forehand and backhand. If you want to get good at this game, having a flexible wrist and perfecting your forehand and backhand play are essential.

Striking the shuttle consists of three parts: the backswing, the forward swing and hit, and the follow-through. Regardless of which stroke is used, the shuttle should be hit high and early. Once you are able to hit the shuttle using the basic swings, you can start perfecting the basic badminton shots: clear, drop, smash and drive.

1. Clear: This shot is the most common and can be offensive, moving your opponent back from the net or defensive, gaining time to improve your own position.

2. Drop: This shot is a slow, gentle shot that falls just over the net into the opponent's forecast.

3. Smash: This shot is a powerful overhead shot used to put away a shuttle that is above the height of the net.

4. Drive: This is a line-drive shot that travels parallel to the ground, passing close over the net.

Strategy of badminton

While it is a great game of social and physical conditioning, don't let badminton fool you. It's also quite a workout for the mind. Strategy is key in the game of badminton, and the game requires constant thinking and planning. Each shot of the shuttle has a purpose, and a good player keeps his or her eye on the entire court at all times.

As you perfect your badminton game, your strategy will naturally mature. However, beginners should adopt a basic strategy of alternating clear and drop shots and adding smashes and drives as the opportunity develops. Try to keep your opponent on the defensive, and remember the following simple points:

1. Always return to the "stance of readiness" position after each shot

2. Be prepared to move in any direction at all times

3. In most cases, overhead shots are the best choice

4. Move the shuttlecock around the court to keep your opponents running

5. Have a purpose with each shot

And, finally, and perhaps most important in any game of skill and strategy, discover your opponents weaknesses and play to it as much as possible.

SHUTTLECOCK

A shuttlecock (also called a bird or birdie) is a high-drag projectile used in the sport of badminton. It has an open conical shape formed by feathers (or a synthetic alternative) embedded into a rounded cork (or rubber) base. Its a half of ball with a net attached

The shuttlecock's shape makes it extremely aerodynamically stable. Regardless of initial orientation, it will turn to fly cork first, and remain in the cork-first orientation.

Name

The name 'shuttlecock' originates in Victorian times, when Badminton first became popular. It is frequently shortened to shuttle. The "shuttle" part of the name was probably derived from its back-and-forth motion during the game, resembling the shuttle of a loom, while the "cock" part of the name was probably derived from the resemblance of the feathers to those on a Rooster.

Specifications

A shuttlecock weighs around 4.75 to 5.50 g (0.168 to 0.194 oz). It has 16 feathers with each feather 70 mm (2.8 in) in length. The diameter of the cork is 25 to 28 mm (0.98 to 1.10 in) and the diameter of the circle that the feathers make is around 54 mm (2.1 in).

Construction and materials

A shuttlecock is formed from 16 or so overlapping feathers, usually goose or duck, embedded into a rounded cork base. The cork is covered with thin leather. To ensure satisfactory flight properties, it is considered preferable to use feathers from right or left wings only in each shuttlecock, and not mix feathers from different wings, as the feathers from different wings are shaped differently.

Feather or Synthetic Shuttlecocks

The feathers are brittle; shuttlecocks break easily and often need to be replaced several times during a game. For this reason, synthetic shuttlecocks have been developed that replace the feathers with a plastic skirt. Players often refer to synthetic shuttlecocks as *plastics* and feathered shuttlecocks as *feathers*.

Feather shuttles need to be properly humidified for at least 4 hours prior to play in order to fly the correct distance at the proper speed and to last longer. Properly humidified feathers flex during play, enhancing the shuttle's speed change and durability. Dry feathers are brittle and break easily, causing the shuttle to wobble. Saturated feathers are 'mushy', making the feather cone narrow too much when strongly hit, which causes the shuttle to fly overly far and fast. Humidification boxes are often used, but a simple moist sponge inserted in the feather end of the closed shuttle tube will work nicely. Water should never touch the cork of the shuttle. Shuttles are tested prior to play to make sure they fly true and at the proper speed, and cover the proper distance. Different weights of shuttles are used to compensate for local atmospheric conditions. Both humidity and height above sea level affect shuttle flight. World Badminton Federation Rules say the shuttle should reach the far doubles service line plus or minus half the width of the tram. According to manufacturers (!) proper shuttle will generally travel from the back line of the court to just short of the long doubles service line on the opposite side of the net, with a full underhand hit from an average player.

The cost of good quality feathers is similar to that of good quality plastics, but plastics are far more durable, typically lasting many matches without any impairment to their flight. Shuttles are easily damaged and should be replaced every three or four games, and sooner if they are damaged and do not fly straight. This interferes with the game, as the impairment on the flight of the shuttle may misdirect the direction of the shuttlecock.

Most experienced and skillful players greatly prefer feathers, and serious tournaments or leagues are always played using feather shuttlecocks of the highest quality. Experienced players generally prefer the "feel" of feathered shuttlecocks and assert that they are able to control the flight of feathers better than that of plastics. In Asia, where feather shuttlecocks are more affordable than in Europe and North America, plastic shuttlecocks are hardly used at all.

The playing characteristics of plastics and feathers are substantially different. Plastics fly more slowly on initial impact, but slow down less towards the end of their flight. While feathers tend to drop straight down on a clear shot, plastics never quite return to a straight drop, falling more on a diagonal. Feather shuttles may come off the strings at speeds in excess of 320 km/h (200 mph) but slow down faster as they drop. For this reason, the feather shuttle makes the game seem faster, but also allows more time to play strokes. Because feather shuttles fly more quickly off the racquet face they also tend to cause less shoulder impact and injury. Shuttle game is a physically rigorous game needing to run, bend quickly and played indoor as either a singles or as doubles game.

THE SCORING SYSTEM IN BADMINT ON

The scoring system in badminton is quite simple, but it can get confusing in doubles. We're going to start with the scoring system for singles, because it's simpler.

Deciding who gets to serve first

In a major tournament, a coin toss is used to decide which side will serve first. In more casual club or league games, you usually just throw the shuttle up in the air, let it land, and see which side it points towards: that side serves first.

Points, games, and matches

Every time you win a rally, you get a point. Starting from zero, the first person to reach 21 points wins the game. In club badminton, this is usually where you stop and choose players for the next game. In standard league or tournament play, however, what really matters is the *match*. A match is the best of three games: you win the match by winning two games. So a match could last either two or three games.

Whenever you win a rally, you also get the next serve. So if your opponent was serving in the last rally, the serve passes to you; if you were serving, you keep on serving.

To win, you need a two-point lead

You have to win the game by at least two points. If the score reaches 20–20, then 21 points are no longer enough to win the game. You need to win two clear points: two points in a row, one after the other.

For example, 22–20 would be a winning score, as would 25–23. But 21–20 would not be enough, and neither would 24–23.

If you reach 30–29, however, you've won the game. 30 points is the upper limit. This rule is intended to prevent games dragging on too long, especially at the top level of play, where excessively long games put athletes at risk of injury.

Always say the server's score first

It's a good habit to say the score to your opponent before starting each rally. It's surprisingly easy to lose track of the score, and saying it between rallies helps prevent disputes.

When you're saying the score, always say the server's score first. So if you are serving and have 10 points to your opponent's 15 points, then the score is 10–15 (not 15–10).

Which side to serve from?

Remember that you have two service courts: one on the right, and one on the left. When the server's score is an even number, he serves from the right service court. When his score is an odd number, he serves from the left service court. For this reason, the right service court is also known as the *even* service court, and the left service court is known as the *odd* service court.

Odd numbers? Even numbers?

- Odd numbers start at 1, and go up by 2
- Even numbers start at 0, and go up by 2

So the odd numbers are 1, 3, 5, 7, 9, 11, 13, and so on. The even numbers are 0, 2, 4, 6, 8, 10, 12, and so on. Even and odd numbers alternate. So if you keep winning rallies, you'll keep serving from a different side each time: right, left, right, left, right, and so on. Because zero is an even number, the game always starts with someone serving from the right (even) service court.

What about the receiver?

The receiver's position is determined not by his own score, but by the server's score. The receiver always stands in the service box diagonally opposite from the server. In other words, both players will be in the even service courts, or both will be in the odd service courts. You can never have one of each (one odd, one even).

Scoring in doubles

The actual *scoring* in doubles is simple: instead of each person winning points, each pair wins points. The part that often confuses people is this: how do you decide who serves, who receives, and which side they should be on? At the start of the game, when the score is 0–0, the serving pair choose who serves for the first rally, and the receiving pair choose who receives.

The even/odd rule still holds. So if the server's score is odd, he will serve from the left court (if even, from the right). Just as for singles, the receiver will stand in the diagonally opposite service court. Whenever the serving side wins a rally, the same person serves again (but from the other service court). The serve does not alternate between the partners: it stays with one person, until the opponents win a rally and get the serve.

Everyone has a service court

To make sense of doubles scoring, you must understand two crucial ideas:

- Every player has a service court, at all times.
- When your partner has one service court, you have the other one.

Let's take an example: you are getting ready to serve from your left service court. So your service court is obvious: it's the box you have to stand inside. Your partner is not serving or receiving, so he doesn't have to stay within one of the service boxes: he can stand anywhere on your court. Nevertheless, we say that your partner has the right service court.

Bizarrely, most people say that your partner is in the right service court. This makes no sense at all, because your partner probably has one foot in each service court!

The same idea applies to the receiving side. In this example, the receiver has the left service court, and his partner has the right service court. Until you serve, the receiver must stay within his service court, but the receiver's partner can stand wherever he wants.

It doesn't matter where you go during the rally

Suppose you serve from the right service court. By the end of the rally, you could easily be standing inside the left service box with your partner standing inside the right box. This has no effect on your service courts for the next rally.

In other words, the service courts are set at the start of the rally. Although you move around during the rally, the service courts don't change. At the end of the rally, you have to remember what your service courts were:

- Who was serving?
- Who was receiving?
- From which side?

Once you remember this, you work out the positions for the next rally.

When you serve and win the rally

Suppose you serve, and then your side wins the rally. For the next rally, you will serve again, but from the other side. In other words: When the serving side win a rally, the server and his partner swap service courts.

Remember that you and your partner must always have different service courts. That's why the server's partner also changes service court here. This change has no effect on the server's partner—he can still stand wherever he wants—but he needs to remember his service court for future rallies.

The receivers never change their service courts. The only way to change service courts is to win a point when your side is serving.

When the receivers win a rally

When the receiving side wins a rally, the serve passes to them. Their service courts do not change from the previous rally. If their new score is odd, then whoever has the left service court will serve; if the score is even, then whoever has the right service court will serve.

Consequences of this system

If you think it through carefully, you can figure out two interesting consequences of this system:

- You never serve to the same person in two consecutive rallies.
- When you win back the serve, the new server is whoever wasn't serving last time.

The rules actually state these consequences explicitly:

Sequence of serving: In any game, the right to serve shall pass consecutively:

- from the initial server who started the game from the right service court
- to the partner of the initial receiver
- to the partner of the initial server
- to the initial receiver
- to the initial server, and so on.

No player shall serve or receive out of turn, or receive two consecutive services in the same game, except as provided in Law 12. (Law 12 is about how you correct mistakes. We'll look at that later.)

It's easy to forget the score or forget which side you were on. When you forget, you can usually use those two facts to help remember.

For example, suppose you have just won back the serve. You know the score is 10–8, but you cannot remember which side you should be. You also know that last time, your partner was serving (not you). Therefore, you must be serving from the right service court.

Similarly, suppose you cannot remember the score. It's either 13–10 or 14–10, and you have just won back the serve. You know that your partner just received in the right service court, and that he was serving last time. This means you must be serving from the left service court, and therefore the score is 13–10.

7

Badminton Strategy

To win in badminton, players need to employ a wide variety of strokes in the right situations. These range from powerful jumping smashes to delicate tumbling net returns. Often rallies finish with a smash, but setting up the smash requires subtler strokes.

For example, a netshot can force the opponent to lift the shuttlecock, which gives an opportunity to smash. If the netshot is tight and tumbling, then the opponent's lift will not reach the back of the court, which makes the subsequent smash much harder to return. Deception is also important. Expert players prepare for many different strokes that look identical, and use slicing to deceive their opponents about the speed or direction of the stroke. If an opponent tries to anticipate the stroke, he may move in the wrong direction and may be unable to change his body momentum in time to reach the shuttlecock.

Singles

The singles court is narrower than the doubles court, but the same length, serve in the single and double back box is out. Since one person needs to cover the entire court, singles tactics are based on forcing the opponent to move as much as possible; this means that singles strokes are normally directed to the corners of the court. Players exploit the length of the court by combining lifts and clears with drop shots and net shots. Smashing is less prominent in singles than in doubles because players are rarely in the ideal position to execute a smash, and smashing often leaves the smasher vulnerable if the smash is returned.

In singles, players will often start the rally with a forehand high serve. Low serves are also used frequently, either forehand or backhand. Flick serves are less common, and drive serves are rare.

At high levels of play, singles demands extraordinary fitness. Singles is a game of patient positional manoeuvring, unlike the all-out aggression of doubles.

Mixed doubles

In mixed doubles, both pairs try to maintain an attacking formation with the woman at the front and the man at the back. This is because the male players are substantially stronger, and can therefore produce smashes that are more powerful. As a result, mixed doubles requires greater tactical awareness and subtler positional play. Clever opponents will try to reverse the ideal position, by forcing the woman towards the back or the man towards the front. In order to protect against this danger, mixed players must be careful and systematic in their shot selection.

At high levels of play, the formations will generally be more flexible: the top women players are capable of playing powerfully from the rearcourt, and will happily do so if required. When the opportunity arises, however, the pair will switch back to the standard mixed attacking position, with the woman in front.

Left Handed Singles

A left-handed player has a natural advantage against a right-handed player. This is because there are more right-handed players in the world (you are not used to playing them). When you play a southpaw, the forehand and backhand are reversed, so that a shot to your right of the court (the backhand of right-handed players) will result in a very powerful smash against you. Because of this, left-handed players tend to have more shots directed to their forehand, and consequently their backhand is not properly trained. Therefore, the main weakness of a southpaw is his backhand. Knowing this, a left-handed player should try to direct most of his shots to the left side of the court. That is because even though it is the forehand of a right-handed person, the return of that shot will also be on your forehand (it is much harder to perform a cross-court shot than a parallel shot). That will ensure that you can keep smashing. It is said that left-handers have better smashes. It is partly true because of the rare angles that a left-hander is capable of producing (a parallel smash on the left side of the court, rather than a slightly angled shot), and also because the feathers on the shuttlecock are placed in a way that favors a left-handed shot (the shuttlecock will have more speed when sliced with a left-handed person's forehand, thus producing a much more powerful smash). Though, a left-handed player himself will be confused when playing a fellow counterpart.

Left handed/Right handed doubles pair

The LH/RH doubles pair is very common at advanced levels of play. That is because they have a distinct advantage over a RH/RH or LH/LH pair. The most notable advantage is that neither side of the court is a weak side. This makes it so that the opposing team have to use more time to think of which side is the backhand and send it there, because against a normal RH/RH pair, you would usually almost always send it to your right side of the court, whilst against a LH/RH pair the weak side changes during the rally. Another advantage is also in the smash of a left-handed player. The feathers of a shuttlecock are placed to have a natural spin, so when slightly slicing the shuttlecock with a left-handed shot, you counter that natural spin which creates drag and produce a faster smash. The same effect goes when a right-handed player slices the shot with his backhand. A very good example of this is Tan Boon Heong, a left-handed player who holds the world record with a 421 km/h smash. Another example is Fu Hai Feng, a left-handed who is renowned for having the hardest smashes in the game. Fu and his right handed partner of Zhang Nan and Cai Yun have won multiple major titles.

BADMINTON - CHAMPION OF CHAMPIONS

Badminton rules were formulated and the sport was standardized in Europe, but most of the prominent players belong to China, Malaysia, and Indonesia. However, the sport is loved and widely played in Europe too.

Players win points by participating in graded tournaments. The World Championships and the Olympics determine the world champion of the year. Players are ranked in all the five categories men's singles, women's singles, men's doubles, women's doubles, and mixed doubles.

Here are some of the prominent players.

Gao Ling

Ling is a Chinese badminton Doubles champion popular for her consistent performance and sporting smile. She won four Olympic medals, two Gold medals in Mixed doubles in 2000 and 2004 Summer Olympics, a Silver medal in Women's doubles in 2004 Summer Olympics, and a Bronze medal in Women's doubles in 2000 Summer Olympics. She also won four World Championship titles, one World Cup, five Uber cup and three Sudirman Cup titles.

Saina Nehwal

The current worlds Women's Singles Champion is from India. She won a Bronze medal in 2012 London Olympics, and is the first Indian to win an Olympic medal for Badminton. She won a Silver medal at 2015 World Championship held at Jakarta. Saina is the first Indian woman to become world number 1 badminton player. In addition, she is the first Indian to win the World Junior Badminton Championships.

Li Lingwei

Li is a former Chinese badminton Champion who dominated the sport during the 80's. She won many Singles as well as Doubles Championships. She won two Gold medals, one Silver medal in Singles, and a Gold medal and a Silver medal in

Doubles at World Championships. She retired in 1989, three years before Badminton was included in the Olympics; so she never won an Olympic medal. She carried the Olympic flag during the opening ceremony of Beijing Olympics in 2008.

Lin Dan

Lin Dan is widely considered to be the best Singles Badminton player. He won two consecutive Olympic Gold medals for men's Singles at 2008 and 2012 Olympics. He is also a five time World Champion, having won the title in 2006, 2007, 2009, 2011, and 2013. He is the first and only player to have won nine major titles in Badminton: Olympics, World Championships, Thomas Cup, World Cup, Super Series Masters Finals, Sudirman Cup, All England Open, Asian Games, and Asian Championships.

Taufik Hidayat

Taufik is a former Indonesian Badminton Champion who won Indonesian Open six times. He is popular for forceful smashes, backhand shots, drop shots, and tricky net shots. He won Olympic Gold for Men's singles in 2004 Olympics and a World Championship in 2005.

Lee Chong Wei

Lee Wei is a Malaysian Badminton champion of Chinese descent. He was ranked as the World's top Champion for 199 consecutive weeks. This man won two Olympic silver medals in 2008 and 2012, three Silver medals in World championships in 2015, 2013, 2011, and a Bronze medal in World Championships in 2005.

Tony Gunawan

He is a former Indonesian Men's Doubles Champion of Chinese descent and has been playing for United States since 2002. He is widely considered to be one of the greatest doubles Badminton players. He won an Olympic Gold at Olympics in 2000 and is the World Champion in Men's Doubles in 2001 and in 2005.

Rudy Hartono

Rudy Hartano is a former Indonesian Badminton star and is one of the greatest men's singles badminton champion in the history of the sport. He won the prestigious All England Championship eight times consecutively from 1968 to 1974 and in 1976, and also the World Championship in 1980.

Morten Frost Hansen

Mortean Hansen, a former Danish badminton player and coach is fondly called Mr. Badminton for he was one of the top three world's best Badminton players for twelve years. He won almost every international Championship, but he only won two Silvers at World Badminton Championships in 1985 and 1987. He dominated the All England Open Badminton Championships, European Championships, and Nordic Championships in the 80's. As a successful coach he steered the Danish team to win over 20 major international titles.

FAULTS

Rallies usually end with a *fault*. Whoever makes the fault loses the rally. For example, hitting the shuttle *out* is a fault: you lose the rally.

Service faults

Badminton has several rules about serving, most of which are meant to limit the advantage that can be gained from a serve. In club badminton play, disputes over the legality of serves are common. It helps to know the rules before you argue over them!

With the exception of delays, breaking any of the following rules is a *fault*. In the case of delays, the umpire will normally warn the players first. If the players continue to delay, then the umpire would usually call a fault.

Definitions

Once the players are ready for the service, the first forward movement of the server's racket head shall be the start of the

service. Once started, the service is delivered when the shuttle
is hit by the server's racket or, in attempting to serve, the
server misses the shuttle. These rules define when the service
starts, and when it is delivered. These definitions get used in
some of the rules below.

Delays

Neither side shall cause undue delay to the delivery of the
service once the server and the receiver are ready for the
service. On completion of the backward movement of the server's
racket head, any delay in the start of the service (Law 9.2) shall
be considered an undue delay. This is really two rules rolled
into one. First, you cannot hold your serve indefinitely, hoping
that the receiver will lose concentration or become
uncomfortable. Similarly, the receiver cannot delay indefinitely.

How long is an undue delay? The rules don't say, because
it's left to the umpire's discretion. In club play, you just have
to be reasonable. I suggest you should not take more than five
seconds to serve (once ready). The second part of the rule is
a convoluted way of saying something quite simple: when
serving, you cannot pause between backswing and forwards
swing. Many club players use this pause to upset the receiver's
timing. That is against the rules: it's a fault.

You might be sceptical about my interpretation here, but
I am following official guidance from *Badminton England*. If
you pause between backswing and forwards swing when serving,
you're breaking the rules. Of course, you don't have to keep the
same *speed* of swing, and you can also serve without using a
backswing at all. Note that this rule also forbids an extremely
slow serving action, because that would constitute an *undue
delay*.

Where the server and receiver must stand

The server and receiver shall stand within diagonally
opposite service courts, without touching the boundary lines of
these service courts. You're not allowed to put your feet on the
lines, when serving or receiving. Note that this rule is only

about *touching* the lines: you may lean forwards or sideways so that your racket is outside the service court.

Keep both feet on the ground

Some part of both feet of the server and the receiver shall remain in contact with the surface of the court in a stationary position from the start of the serve until the service is delivered.

Both feet must stay on the ground until the server contacts the shuttle. Only *some part* of each foot has to stay on the ground; this allows you to shift your weight and even turn your body (as in a forehand high serve). You may not drag a foot along the floor, however.

Hit the base of the shuttle first

The server's racket shall initially hit the base of the shuttle. This rule seems incongruous unless you know its history. It was introduced to prevent players using a particular style of low serve. The serve was called the *Sidek*serve or *S-serve*, after the Sidek brothers who popularised it in the 1980s. It was mainly used as a backhand serve.

The S-serve involved slicing sideways across the feathers of an inverted shuttle, making it spin chaotically so that the receiver had difficulty controlling his return. The S-serve was so effective that many people felt it was ruining the game; eventually, the serve was banned by introducing rule 9.1.4 (above).

Tournament video footage of the S-serve is hard to find, but here's one examplewhere both sides are mainly using S-serves (a good example is at 7:41). Note the wild, downwards-swerving path of many serves. The receivers make a large number of errors, and rarely succeed in attacking the S-serves.

Although the S-serve is against the rules, other spinning serves are not. You may still slice the serve, and you may even hit the feathers, providing you hit the base first. These techniques may cause the shuttle to spin, wobble, or swerve, although the effect is far less dramatic than an S-serve.

Serve from below the waist

The whole shuttle shall be below the server's waist at the instant of being hit by the server's racket. The waist shall be considered an imaginary line round the body, level with the lowest part of the server's bottom rib.

This is an important rule: it's the one that prevents you from playing a smash as your serve! Note that the waist is not the same as the line of your shorts: it's actually the lowest part of your ribcage. To judge how high you can serve from, feel for your lowest rib: the shuttle has to be below this.

The angle of the server's racket

The shaft of the server's racket at the instant of hitting the shuttle shall be pointing in a downward direction. At first, this seems an unnecessary rule. We already have rule 9.1.5 to enforce a height limit; why do we need another one?

This rule is useful because it prevents players from applying heavy top-spin to their drive serves. These serves travel fast and flat, and can actually swerve *downwards* after passing the net so that they reach the receiver below net height. They are almost impossible to attack.

Drive serves can be perfectly legal, but this rule ensures that all legal drive serves will travel upwards as they pass the net—making them vulnerable to attack by an alert receiver.

No stop-start serving

The movement of the server's racket shall continue forwards from the start of the service (Law 9.2) until the service is delivered (Law 9.3). Many servers like to shake their racket back-and-forth behind the shuttle, as an attempt to disturb the receiver's timing. That is a fault.

This rule, ensures that the service action must be one continuous movement with no double-action feints. To be precise, you are allowed to serve with either of these actions:

- One backswing immediately followed by one forwards swing

- One forwards swing on its own (no backswing)

Where you have to serve

The flight of the shuttle shall be upwards from the server's racket to pass over the net so that, if not intercepted, it shall land in the receiver's service court (i.e. on or within the boundary lines).

A serve that hits the line is *in*. The rule *appears* to suggest that, even if the receiver hits it back, a serve that was travelling *out* should be faulted. That is a misinterpretation of the rule: notice that the rule says shall land, not would land!

So the rule is technically correct, but it's still badly worded. Some silly stuff: even if you were three metres tall and could hit a serve downwards, it would still be against the rules, because the serve must travel upwards. You also are not allowed to use some sneaky trick serve that swerves around the sides of the net posts!

No second chances

In attempting to serve, the server shall not miss the shuttle. If you miss the shuttle on serving, you lose the rally. I recommend practising your serve more.

Although it's not explicitly mentioned anywhere in the rules, you also don't get a second serve. This is different from tennis, where the server gets two attempts to put the ball inside the service court.

Faults during the rally

Hitting the shuttle to the wrong place

[It shall be a fault] if in play, the shuttle:

- lands outside the boundaries of the court (i.e. not on or within the boundary lines);
- passes through or under the net;
- fails to pass over the net;

These are fairly obvious. Your shot must travel over the net, not underneath, around, or through it; and it must land inside your opponent's court (unless he hits it back).

If the shuttle lands on the line, it's *in*. Only the first contact between the shuttle and the floor counts. Shuttles often hit the line and then bounce out; this counts as *in*.

When the shuttle touches something before reaching the floor

[It shall be a fault] if in play, the shuttle:

- touches the ceiling or side walls;
- touches the person or dress of a player;
- touches any other object or person outside the court;

(Where necessary on account of the structure of the building, the local badminton authority may, subject to the right of veto of its Member Association, make bye-laws dealing with cases in which a shuttle touches an obstruction.)

You lose the rallly if you hit the shuttle into the ceiling or walls. You also lose the rally if the shuttle touches you or your clothing. The last rule is just a stuffy way of acknowledging that many badminton courts are not perfect. For example, many courts have beams or girders crossing low above them. Most clubs decide to play a let when the shuttle hits a beam. This is standard practice, and I recommend it.

You cannot claim a let for hitting the ceiling, however. Otherwise, whenever you were losing the rally, you could just hit the shuttle up to the ceiling and start again! Surprisingly, the rules do not specify a minimum ceiling height. Playing badminton with a low ceiling ruins the game, as it makes defensive shots ineffective. In practice, all major tournaments use very high ceilings, but some local or regional venues do not.

Double hits

[It shall be a fault] if in play, the shuttle:

- is caught and held on the racket and then slung during the execution of a stroke;

- is hit twice in succession by the same player. However, a shuttle hitting the head and the stringed area of the racket in one stroke shall not be a fault;
- is hit by a player and the player's partner successively;

With a little practice, it's possible to catch the shuttle with your racket, using a scooping motion. For obvious reasons, you're not allowed to do this during a rally.

Similarly, you may not hit the shuttle twice, on your own or with a partner—for example, first hitting it up above net height, and then smashing it down!

Note that a bad contact is not a fault. Many players, especially older ones, call no shot when they have made a bad contact—either hitting just the frame, or hitting both the frame and the strings. This is not a fault, and the rally should continue.

Hitting the net or invading the opponent's court

[It shall be a fault] if in play, a player:

- touches the net or its support with racket, person or dress;
- invades an opponent's court over the net with racket or person except that the striker may follow the shuttle over the net with the racket in the course of a stroke after the initial point of contact with the shuttle is on the striker's side of the net;
- invades an opponent's court under the net with racket or person such that an opponent is obstructed or distracted;

If you touch the net or the posts, you lose the rally. This commonly happens with net kills: if the shuttle is tight to the net, it can be hard to play a net kill without hitting the net with your racket.

You are not allowed to reach over the net to play your shot. Provided you make contact with the shuttle on your side, however, your racket may then pass over the net during your follow-through action.

It's hard to be sure what the rules intend for edge cases, such as a tight brush net kill where the contact point is on your side but the top of your racket is intruding (just slightly) over the net. Even in officiated tournaments, these calls are made by eye, without the aid of video replays or electronic sensors (although video replays are sometimes used when the call is disputed). In practice, the court officials have a hard enough time judging whether the contact point was okay. To spot these edge cases accurately is beyond human ability.

In other words, I wouldn't worry about it. Just make sure that you contact the shuttle on your side.

When lunging forwards to retrieve a tight drop or net shot, players often put a foot under the net. This is not a fault unless you obstruct or distract the opponent—for example, by treading on his foot!

Obstructions and distractions

[It shall be a fault] if in play, a player:

- obstructs an opponent, i.e. prevents an opponent from making a legal stroke where the shuttle is followed over the net;
- deliberately distracts an opponent by any action such as shouting or making gestures;

Remember that you are allowed to follow-through with your racket over the net, providing you made contact on your side. If your opponent obstructs this—such as putting his racket in the way so that you would be forced to hit it—then you win the rally.

Note that your opponent is allowed to put his racket in the path of the shuttle. He is not allowed to block your stroke, but he is allowed to block your shot. It's a subtle distinction: your *stroke* is the movement of your racket; your shot is the movement of the shuttle.

Deliberate distractions are not allowed. There's a fine line here: the rule does not prohibit shouting (e.g. when you smash) or expressing yourself through gestures (e.g. a clenched fist after winning a point); but it does prohibit using these to distract your opponent.

BADMINTON SINGLES STRA TEGY

The new scoring system has led to some players re-thinking their singles strategies. This maybe because at the end of each rally a point is now scored, so having the serve is less important. Here we explain in more detail the rules and how to gain an advantage.

If a player wins the coin toss they can choose:
- A side of the net to start from
- Whether to serve
- Whether to receive

If the opponent wins the toss and they choose the side, then the other player still has the choice of whether to serve or receive. Or if they choose to serve or receive the other player can choose the side to start from. What to do: Having won the toss under the new scoring system a player may prefer to choose a side to start from instead of serving or receiving. This is especially true if there is a clear bad and good side to the court. Differences can include:
- The court surface
- The background
- Reflections
- Ceiling or wall lighting
- Placement of windows

If there are differences it is advised that a player chooses the bad side first for a few reasons. If a player wins the first set from the bad side then they have a good chance to win the next set and the match from the good side. Playing from the good side should be easier, which will increase a players confidence, maybe upping their performance when they go back to the bad side for the first part of the third set if the match goes that far. Also choosing the bad side first will mean if the match does go to the third set they will finish on the good side

What to do: If an opponent wins the toss and selects the bad side, the other player should opt to receive the serve first. This is because of the new scoring system making it much easier to win points when receiving the serve. If the server now fails to hit the shuttle into the service area a point is awarded to the receiving player. In the old system if this happened the serve would just switch to the other player and there would be no change in the score.

The serve is often a defensive shot because it has to be hit from below the waist, meaning it has an upward trajectory to travel over the net. This allows the receiving player to attack and control the rally. However if serving is a strong part of a players game they may decide to go first. Every player is different and should choose the option they are most comfortable with.

Changes to the Game: Some players and coaches think the game is now more conservative because all players know that with 1 error they will lose a point whether they are serving or not. So they may be hitting the shuttle with less power and directing it more towards the center of the court to avoid hitting it out. This makes the rallies longer because the shuttles are easier to reach.

Under the old method the more talented player would win comfortably because they could afford to go for the more risky shots when they were serving, because even if they missed, they wouldn't lose a point, just the serve. This makes each game closer and helps the less able player to score some points.

Top tips

Badminton is a very tactical and strategic game. Basically you need to keep returning the shuttle for longer than the opponent whilst trying to outwit them, and move them around the court using a variety of shots, with disguise if possible. Being a quick thinker is important to make decisions about what shot to play, in the limited time players have to return the shuttle effectively.

For beginners to badminton the main points to focus on are:

- Hitting the shuttle consistently high and deep to give time to recover.
- Try to aim shots to the opponents weaker side (usually backhand), to give the advantage off a weak return.
- Try to place shots before adding more power, because more power will usually result in more errors.
- Try to keep the opponent on the move as much as possible and not play me to you badminton. This is when two players just stand in the center of the court and hit the shuttle back and forth between them. Try moving the opponent from the net to the back and from the forehand to backhand side to fatigue them quicker.
- Keep winning, keep playing the same way
- Keep losing change the style of play
- Try to change the speed of play, by mixing up shots. For example hit some slower shots, such as, drop shots and net shots, with faster shots in between, such as, smashes, and drives.
- Always play to personal strengths and try to exploit the opponents weaknesses.

Master all of these points then start to add disguise to shots or attempt to incorporate more advanced strokes.

- Always believe winning is an option. If players go into a match thinking they will lose they almost certainly will.
- Play to strengths

- Always try to go back to base (centre court) after every shot.
- A deep and accurate serve is vital.
- Always keep an eye on the shuttle
- Try to find weaknesses in the opponent as early as possible and continue to exploit them.
- Keep the opponent guessing and moving
- Keep playing and trying until the end, anything could happen.
- Use deception wherever possible
- Practice, practice, practice
- Keep calm at all times do not encourage the opponent with signs of disappointment or anger.
- Play against better players to improve.

BADMINTON DOUBLES STRA TEGY

A teams positioning in doubles is determined by both teams shots, however there are certain times in a match when both teams should be in specific positions. Here we explain doubles positioning as well as some top tips to give you and your partner an advantage.

Doubles positioning

On Serve: When a player is serving both the server and receiver should be in the up position just behind the service line. The other player on each team then takes up the back position near the mid court. This happens because both teams want to gain an early advantage in the rally and try and force their opponents into hitting a defensive stroke.

Receiving a high serve: When receiving a high serve, the receiver should move to the back of the court to return the serve and their partner should go to the front of the court, because a high serve gives the receiving team a chance to attack.

Hitting a high serve: When hitting a high serve switch to the side by side formation because the shuttle has been hit up giving the opponents a chance to attack.

When attacking: The up and back system is usually used because having a player at the front is intimidating, and they can angle the shuttle down more from that position to make it difficult for the opposing team to return the shuttle. A team should go on the attack when their opponents hit a shuttle up.

When defending: Players move into a side by side system because if the other team are attacking they are more likely to aim the shuttle down at the mid court. So being side by side each player on the defending team only has to defend one side of the court instead of the whole width of it, if they stayed in the up and back position. A team should move into this position when their opponents hit the shuttle down or they play an upward shot themselves.

Top tips

The following points are important to master if a team wants to be successful in doubles matches.

- Always believe the team can win. If a team goes into a match thinking they will lose they almost certainly will.
- Play to the teams strengths
- Remember which position each player is supposed to be in within the team.
- A short and accurate serve is vital.
- Always keep an eye on the shuttle
- Try to find weaknesses in opponents as early as possible and continue to exploit them.
- Keep the opponents guessing and moving
- Keep playing and trying until the end, anything could happen.
- Use deception wherever possible
- Practice, practice, practice

- Keep calm at all times do not encourage the opponents with signs of disappointment or anger.
- Test the team against better players, the team should raise their game.
- Communicate with each other as much as possible

Doubles strategy

The new scoring system has led to some players re-thinking their doubles strategies. This maybe because at the end of each rally a point is now scored, so having the serve is less important. The team that wins the coin toss can choose:

- A side of the net to start from
- Whether to serve
- Whether to receive

If the opponents win the toss and they choose the side, then the other team still have the choice of whether to serve or receive. Or if they choose to serve or receive the other team can choose the side to start from.What to do: If a team wins the toss under the new scoring system they may prefer to choose a side to start from instead of receiving. In doubles a team should never opt to serve first, the first choice should be to take the bad side. Differences can include:

- The court surface
- The background
- Reflections
- Ceiling or wall lighting
- Placement of windows

There are a few reasons why a team should choose the bad side. If a team win the first set from the bad side then they have a good chance to win the next set and the match from the good side. Playing from the good side should be easier, which will increase the confidence, maybe upping the performance when going back to the bad side for the first part of the third set if the match goes that far.

Also choosing the bad side first will mean if the match does go to the third set a team will finish on the good side.

What to do: If the opponents win the toss and selects the bad side, opt to receive the serve first. This is because of the new scoring system making it much easier to win points when receiving the serve. If the server now fails to hit the shuttle into the service area a point is awarded to the receiving player. In the old system if this happened the serve would just switch to the other player and there would be no change in the score.

The serve is often a defensive shot because it has to be hit from below the waist, meaning it has an upward trajectory to travel over the net. This allows the receiving player to attack and control the rally. However if serving is a strong part of a players game they may decide to go first.

Serving First: If a team does serve first, because of the rule in doubles about designating which player is starting from each side, the team may want to put their best server starting the match, therefore being on the even side.

Receiving First: If a team is receiving first then they should put their best receiver in the even court to try and win the first rally.

Impact of the new scoring system: In doubles it seems the new scoring does not have such a great effect as it does in singles. The only real change that has been noticed are scores being closer, and rallies being longer due to the more conservative play.

8

Badminton Glossary

A

Alley - The 18-inch section of the badminton court between singles and doubles sidelines.

Around-the-head shot - An advanced shot where a player reaches around the head to his backhand side to strike the shuttle with the forehand. This often leaves the player off-balanced and vulnerable.

Attacking (Driving) clear - A variation of a clear shot achieved by driving the bird harder and with a flatter trajectory.

B

Back alley - The area on both ends of the court between the singles and doubles service line.

Backcourt - The back third portion of the court around the long-service lines.

Backhand - A basic shot where a player reaches to his non-dominant side and strikes the shuttle with the backside of the racquet. This is generally the weakest shot by a player and is taken with his back facing the net.

Backhand grip - There are many variations of the backhand grip, but it is essentially a change in grip to help a player strike the shuttle with his backhand.

Balk (Feint) - A serve that deceives an opponent and usually results in a poor return.

Base (Center) position - Sometimes referred to as the home or center position, this is the spot a player returns to after striking the shuttle.

Baseline - The back line at both ends of the court that runs parallel to the net.

Bird (Birdie) - Commonly used name for the shuttlecock.

Block - A quick return of either a smash or a drive that requires a small, swift flick of the wrist to drop the shuttle just over the net.

C

Carry - An illegal shot where the shuttle is caught, held on to, and then slung during the execution of a stroke.

Center line - The line that runs through the middle of the court and perpendicular to the net separating the service courts.

Clear - A basic shot where a player contacts the bird high and arches it over the opponent toward the other baseline.

Cork - The head of the shuttle that is made of cork.

Court - The overall area of play defined by the outer boundaries.

Cross-court shot - Any shot that crosses the center line. Cross-court can be prefixed for any basic shot.

D

Doubles - A mode of playing in which one team of two players competes against another team of two players.

Drive - A basic shot where a player contacts the shuttle around head or shoulder height and propels the shuttle hard and with a flat trajectory.

Drop - A basic shot where a player uses finesse to pass the shuttle low over the net. The shot typically lands before the short-service line.

E

Event - The disciplines in which a player can compete in tournament play. The standard events are men's/women's singles, men's/women's doubles, and mixed Doubles.

F

Fast drop - A variation of a drop shot that has a player strike the shuttle harder to give the opponent less time to react. The resulting shot will have a flatter trajectory, causing the shuttle to land farther from the net.

Fault - A violation of rules during play.

Flick - A swift rotation of the forearm and wrist used to generate lots of power in a short amount of time. This technique is often used to disguise fast, deep shots as slow drop shots.

Flick serve - An advanced service shot taken from the backhand position and arched over the opponent toward the long-service line. This shot requires a developed forearm and wrist to generate the power and quickness to catch the receiver off guard.

Flight - The difficulty or skill level of an event in a tournament usually designated by the letters A, B, C and D, with A being the most-advanced level.

Foot fault - A service fault made by a player in which he oversteps the boundary of the service court.

Forecourt - The front third portion of the court around the short-service lines.

Forehand (Handshake) grip - The standard grip used for most forehand shots, sometimes referred to as the "handshake" grip because of its likeness to "shaking hands" with the racquet.

Frame - The portion of the racquet that outlines the head and secures the strings.

Frame shot (Dink) - Any shot that has a player contact the shuttle with the frame of the racquet.

Front-back - The attacking position in doubles where both players are in the middle with one in the fore-to-midcourt and the other in the backcourt.

Funky doubles - A term used to designate a less constricting form of doubles play offered in some tournaments. In general, this event allows for any combination of skill levels and genders with a few exceptions defined by each tournament.

G

Game ("Point") - Either word should be announced, out of courtesy, when serving for a game-winning point.

Game (Set) - A 21-point series with a required two-point margin of victory. If a game goes past 21 points it ends when one team either goes up by two points or reaches 30.

Grip - The material over the handle of racquet that can be changed for better comfort and control.

H

Hairpin net shot - A variation of a net drop that has a trajectory similar to that of a hairpin. The shuttle is contacted low and hugs the net on both sides to create an equally difficult shot for the opponent.

Half-court shot - A shot directed at midcourt and normally achieved with a drop or drive.

Handle - The end portion of a racquet, opposite the head, where a player takes hold.

Head - The portion of the racquet that is comprised of the frame and the strings.

High clear - A variation of a clear shot that arches high toward the opponent's baseline. This shot is intended to allow a team or player to reset defensively or to disrupt the opponent's timing.

I

Interval (Break) - A 60-second period of rest that occurs when the score reaches 11 for the first time in a game. There is also a 120-second break in between games. Players are permitted to leave the court during this time.

J

Jump smash - An advanced shot where a player is airborne while smashing the shuttle.

K

Kill - A quick, downward shot that ends a rally.

L

Let - A legitimate stoppage of play that allows a rally to be replayed.

Lift - A variation of a clear shot that is produced by an underhand stroke and arched high to allow time for better defensive positioning.

Line judge - A pre-approved, unbiased individual responsible for determining whether or not shots land inside of the boundaries.

Long-service line - The back line for singles matches or the line 2.5 feet inwards for doubles matches. Serves may not land past these lines for the corresponding games.

Lunge - A vital part of footwork that has a player reach with his racquet-side leg to strike the shuttle.

M

Match - Comprised of a best two-out-of-three-games format in tournament play.

Match ("Point") - Either word should be announced, out of courtesy, when serving for a match-winning point.

Men's doubles - A match comprised of two teams with two male players on each team.

Midcourt - The middle third portion of the court in between the short-service and long-service lines.

Mixed doubles - A match comprised of two teams with one male and one female player on each team.

N

Net - The piece of equipment held up by two poles and used to separate teams on each side.

Net drop - A basic shot where a player simultaneously receives a drop shot and returns one.

Net fault - When any player touches the net with his racquet, body, or apparel during play.

O

Overhand shot - Any shot taken with a downward arm and wrist motion.

P

Panhandle grip - A variation of the natural grip in which the palm is facing the fat part of the handle with the thumb and fingers grasping the thinner sides. This grip is normally used for drive shots and allows greater range with forehand drives.

Passing shot - Any shot that passes behind an opponent and forces him to reach back to return the shot.

Plastic shuttle - A type of shuttle with a skirt made of plastic.

Push shot - An overhand shot taken in the mid or forecourt and directed toward the opponent's mid or backcourt. The shot is either a drive or drop relying on its quick return rather than its power.

R

Racquet - The piece of equipment used to strike the shuttle. A racquet is comprised of a racquet head, strings, a t-joint, a shaft, and a handle. Racquets can be made of wood, steel, and titanium, but are commonly made with carbon fiber/ graphite.

Rally - The series of shots that takes place between service and the end of play.

Rally-scoring - The manner of scoring in which a point is awarded for every rally.

Rotation - The movement or interaction that allows doubles partners to attack or defend effectively as a team.

S

Scorekeeper - A pre-approved, unbiased individual who is responsible for scoring a match.

Serve (Service) - The shot that starts a rally.

Service court - The area in which a serve is legally allowed to land. The singles service court is longer and narrower, while the doubles service court is shorter and wider.

Service fault - Any violation or illegal tactic that occurs during service for either team.

Service judge - A pre-approved, unbiased individual who is responsible for calling service faults.

Short-service line - The service line that is closest to the net and runs parallel to it.

Shuffle (Skip) - A primary part of footwork technique that has a player slide his feet to move around the court.

Shuttlecock (Shuttle) - The object that is hit back and forth in badminton.

Side-by-side - The defensive doubles position where both players are at midcourt and on either side of the center line.

Singles - A mode of playing with one player on each side. The court is defined by the inner sideline and baseline.

Skirt - The part of the shuttle that is either plastic or feather and fans out like a skirt.

Slice - An advanced shot that is achieved by contacting the shuttle with the racquet head at an angle noticeably different than the path of the shuttle. This "slicing" motion is sometimes used to create misdirection to trick the opponent.

Smash - A basic shot where the shuttle is contacted high and directed downward at a sharp angle with immense speed. This shot is typically steeper than a drive shot.

Strings - The thin, synthetic pieces of material that are weaved through the frame and used to propel the shuttle.

T

Throat (T-joint) - The section of the racquet that connects the head to the shaft. Older, lower-end models typically have a visibly separate t-joint, while newer, higher-end models incorporate it into the racquet.

Tumble drop shot - A variation of a drop shot that causes the shuttle to flip, end over end. This maneuver makes the shuttle more difficult for the opponent to return.

U

Underhand - Any shot taken with an upward arm and wrist motion.

Bibliography

Adams, Bernard: *The Badminton Story*, BBC Books, 1980.

Adams, Ronald C. : *Games, Sports and Exercises for the Physically Disabled*, Philadelphia, Lea & Febiger, 1991.

Andersen, M. B.: *Doing Sport Psychology.* Champaign, Il: Human Kinetics, 2000.

Baitsch, H.: *The Scientific View of Sport and Drugs.* New York: Springer-Verlag, 1972.

Bhardwaj, Ramesh : *The Coach and Sports Injuries*, Sports Publication, Delhi, 2011.

Boga, Steve: *Badminton*, Paw Prints, 2008.

Caswell, Lucy Shelton: *Guide to Sources in Sports History,* New York, Greenwood Press, 1989.

Chisholm, Hugh: *"Badminton (game)"*, Cambridge University Press, 1911.

Connors, M.; Dupuis, D.L.; Morgan, B.: *The Olympics Factbook: A Spectator's Guide to the Winter and Summer Games*, Visible Ink Press, 1991.

Creswdl, J. W.: *Qualitative Inquiry and Research Design: Choosing among Traditions.* Thousand Oaks: Sage, 1998.

Davis, K. : *Adapted Physical Education for Students with Autism*, Springfield, IL: Charles C. Thomas, 1990.

Downey, Jake; Downey, Jason Charles: *Better Badminton for All*, Pelham Books, 1982.

Eisenberg, Christiane and Pierre Lanfranchi: : *Football History: International Perspectives*; Special Issue, Historical Social Research, 2006.

Elliott, James: *Sports: Politics and Public Sector Management*, London, Retailed, 1997.

Gay L. R.: *Educational Research Competencies for Analyses and Application.* Ohio: Charles E. Merill, 1976.

Grice, Tony: *Badminton: Steps to Success*, Human Kinetics, 2008.

Guillain, Jean-Yves: *Badminton: An Illustrated History*, Publibook, 2004.

Guttman, A.: *Sports Spectators*. New York: Columbia University Press, 1986.

Hall, C Michael *Sports Planning: Policies, Processes and relationships*, Harlow, Prentice Hall, 2000.

Herzog, Brad: *Hoopmania: The Book of Basketball History and Trivia*. Rosen Pub. Group. 2003.

Jennings, Gayle: *Sports Economics: Research and Development*, Chichester, Wiley, 2001.

Kim, Wangdo: *An Analysis of the Biomechanics of Arm Movement During a Badminton Smash (PDF)*, Nanyang Technological University, 2002.

Kolah, A.: *Maximizing the Value of Sponsorship*. London: Sports Business Croup, 2003.

Lieberman, L. : *'Games and Activities for Individuals with Sensory Impairments'*, in Grosse, Reston, VA, AAHPERD Publications, 1993.

Lieberman, L. : *'Games and Activities for Individuals with Sensory Impairments'*, in Grosse, Reston, VA, AAHPERD Publications, 1993.

Manoj Thomas: *New Era of Sports Management*, Khel Sahitya Kendra, Delhi, 2007.

Michael, R.M. : *A Handbook of Sports Chronobiology*, Cyber Tech Publications, Delhi, 2011.

Murthy, J. Krishna : *Administration and Organisation of Physical Education and Sports*, Commonwealth, Delhi, 2005.

Nafziger, JAR, *International Sports Law*, 1988, New York: Transnational

Naismith, James: *Basketball: its origin and development*. University of Nebraska Press. 1941.

Paul Heyer: *Sports Chronology*, Boston, Allyn and Bacon, 2003.

Rao, Bhaskara : *Sports Management*, APH, Delhi, 2003.

Ronald C. : *Games, Sports and Exercises for the Physically Disabled*, Philadelphia, Lea & Febiger, 1991.

Ruddy, J: *Sports Tourism Destination Planning*, Dublin, Dublin Institute of Technology, 2002.

Index

□□□

CPSIA information can be obtained
at www.ICGtesting.com
Printed in the USA
LVHW031725031220
673320LV00061B/1634

9 789352 976928